THE HOT SAUCE COLLECTOR'S GUIDE

A book for collectors, retailers, manufacturers, and lovers of all things hot

Jennifer Trainer Thompson

Ten Speed Press
Berkeley, California

Three years ago, I took a picture of my hot sauce collection and turned it into a poster. That poster was followed by several other hot sauce posters, and then THE GREAT HOT SAUCE BOOK. Since then, I've received thousands of inquiries — by phone, fax, e-mail, and post — from people who have gone to great lengths to track me down and request more information about hot sauces: Where can they find a particular sauce? Is so-and-so out of business? Who sells sauces in Arkansas . . . or New York . . . or England? Where is that bar in the mountains that makes the killer Armageddon Sauce? This book answers those questions, and is densely packed with practical information — everything you need to know to build a terrific hot sauce collection. So get sauced, and enjoy.

—*Jennifer Trainer Thompson*

With special thanks to Dennis Hayes

Ten Speed Press
P.O. Box 7123
Berkeley, California 94707

Cover design by Toni Tajima
Text design by Jeff Brandenburg

Library of Congress Cataloging-in-Publication Data

Thompson, Jennifer Trainer.
        The hot sauce collector's guide : a book for collectors, retailers,
    manufacturers, and lovers of all things hot / by Jennifer Trainer Thompson.
            p.   cm.
        Includes index.
        ISBN 0-89815-924-5
        1. Hot pepper sauces—Directories.   I. Title.
    TX819.H66T493 1996
    664'.58—dc21   96-38083
                                                                            CIP

Printed in Canada
First printing, 1997

1   2   3   4   5   /   01   00   99   98   97

CONTENTS

Hot Challenge

Do you have a Blazin' Saddle? How about Inner Beauty? Do you reach for the Ultimate Burn (or Asbirin) after you try Capital Punishment? Send proof that your sauce collection exceeds 500 sauces and not only will I send you an autographed hot sauce poster, but your name will be immortalized on the Wall of Flame prominently displayed at Ten Speed Press, that publishing paean to capsicum capriciousness. Mail photo — or whatever — to:

Jennifer Thompson
c/o Wall of Flame
Ten Speed Press
P. O. Box 7123
Berkeley CA, 94707

BLUE POSTER

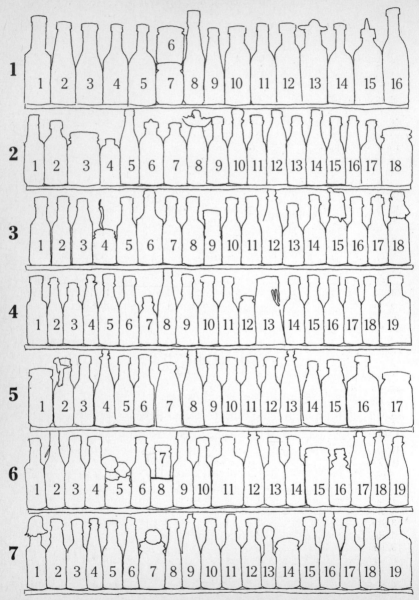

Key to Blue Poster

These sauces are listed alphabetically in Section I.

Row 1
1. Lingham's
2. Matouk's
3. Evadney's
4. Creole "Shut…"
5. Louisiana Gold
6. Rebel Fire #1
7. Rebel Fire #3
8. Sriraja Factory
9. Bufalo Jalapeño
10. Gecko Jalapeño
11. Sylvia's
12. Andy's
13. Three Banditos
14. Texas Champagne
15. Huy Fong Tuong
16. Oochie's Redneck

Row 2
1. Coyote Cocina Smoky
2. Pee Wee's Cajun
3. Don Alfonso
4. Clancy's Fancy
5. Firey Louisiana
6. Miz Grazi's
7. Bill Wharton's
8. Adobe Milling
9. Dave's Insanity
10. Cholula Sauce
11. Hot Lava
12. Sho Nuff
13. Another Bloody Day
14. Chef Hans'
15. Uncle Billy's
16. Pepper Creek
17. Panola Jalapeño
18. Crazy Cajun

Row 3
1. Lotta Hotta
2. Jump Up & Kiss Me
3. Durkee Red Hot
4. Red Dog Nuclear
5. Mrs. Dog's
6. La Anita
7. Panola Gourmet
8. Uno

9. I Am On Fire!
10. Hot as Hell
11. Melinda's
12. Windmill
13. Panola Extra
14. El Yucateco
15. Tabasco
16. Ass Kickin'
17. Trinidad Extra Hot
18. Hawaiian Passion
19. Desert Fire

Row 4
1. Papa Joe
2. Ana Belly
3. Montezuma Devil's
4. West Indies Creole
5. Dilijan Liquid Spice
6. Island Treasure Papaya
7. Ieeowch!!!
8. Flame Louisiana
9. 911 Hot Sauce
10. Coyote Cocina Howlin'
11. Capital Punishment
12. Scorned Woman
13. same as above
14. Texas Tears
15. The Mex
16. Island Heat
17. Satan's Revenge
18. Barbados Jack
19. Inner Beauty

Row 5
1. Hell in a Bottle
2. Hellfire & Damnation
3. Bandana's
4. Bat's Brew
5. Spitfire
6. Caribe Cookery
7. not labeled
8. A.B.
9. Craig's HOT!
10. Jamaica Hell Fire
11. Heatwave
12. Sontava!
13. Panola Extra Hot

14. Evadney's Fire Water
15. Andre's Rouge
16. not labeled
17. Religious Experience

Row 6
1. Devil Drops
2. Dewey Beach Fire
3. Jamaica Hell Fire
4. Hawaiian Passion Fire
5. Pili Hot Pepper
6. Grand Anse Moko
7. Harissa
8. Harissa Dea
9. Busha Browne's
10. Dr. J's
11. Inner Beauty
12. Vampfire
13. Montezuma Wild
14. Pickapeppa Sauce
15. Santa Fe Exotic
16. Macarico Piri-Piri
17. Louisiana The Perfect
18. Panola Cajun
19. Fish Camp Habañero

Row 7
1. Sunny Caribbee
2. Montezuma Aztec
3. Hot Stuff Jab-Jab
4. Crystal
5. Flying Burrito
6. Casa Fiesta
7. Virgin Fire Pineapple
8. Shotgun Willie's
9. Arizona Gunslinger
10. Last Rites
11. Habañero from Hell
12. Outerbridge's Original
13. Cholula
14. Stonewall Salsa
15. Try Me Tiger
16. Panola 10 Point
17. Mad Dog Liquid Fire
18. Try Me Cajun
19. Isla Vieques Caribe

v

RED POSTER

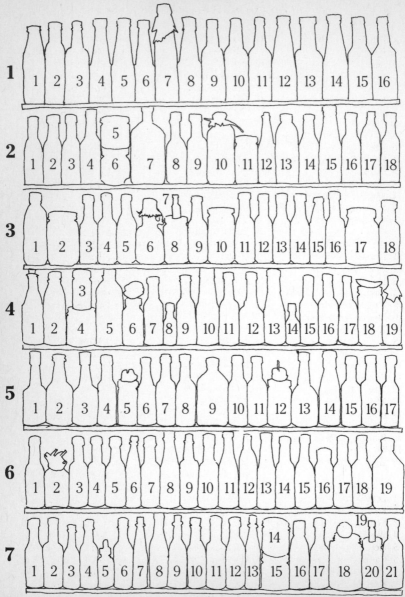

Key to Red Poster

These sauces are listed alphabetically in Section I.

Row 1
1. E.M.G. Local Pepper
2. HP Chilli Sauce
3. Mrs. Tull's Homemade
4. Chief Trinidad
5. Bowman's
6. La Guaca-Maya
7. Ring of Fire
8. Cholimex
9. California Perfect Pepper
10. Achiote Indian Sauce
11. Ayla's Organics
12. Gunsam's
13. Gib's Mo' Hotter
14. Special Pepper
15. Rowena's Red
16. Gator Hammock Gator

Row 2
1. Lotta Hotta
2. Virgin Islands
3. Liquid Sky
4. Busha Browne's
5. Dave's Temp. Insanity
6. So Damned Insane
7. The S Bend
8. Tabasco Jalapeño
9. Isla Vieques Sweet
10. not labeled
11. Freddy's
12. Goya Hot Sauce
13. La Botanera
14. Iguana Red Pepper
15. La Victoria Taco Sauce
16. Batten Island
17. Tamazula
18. Triple Barn Burner

Row 3
1. Lottie's True
2. Rio Diablo
3. Key West Really
4. Westlow's
5. Hot Buns
6. Caribbee Pepper
7. Panda Premium
8. Rica Red Hot Pepper

9. Evadney's
10. Margaret's
11. Outerbridge's
12. Trader Rick
13. Montezuma Toltec
14. Grace Original
15. Jamaica Best
16. Hot Wings
17. Cajun Rush

Row 4
1. Trappey's Mexi-Pep
2. Pick-a-Pepper
3. S.O.B.
4. Bourbon Street
5. Windmill Hot
6. Red Dog Tavern
7. Pirate's Blend
8. Erica's
9. Vito's Hot Flash
10. Lee Kum Kee
11. Chombo Sauce
12. Flam-n-John
13. Pico Pica
14. Grand Anse #5
15. Baron West Indian
16. Tapatio Salsa
17. Juanita's
18. Hell and Beyond
19. Habañero! HOT!

Row 5
1. Hot Ketchita
2. No Joke
3. Mild Ketchita
4. Susie's Original
5. Grand Anse Peppa-Po
6. Trappey's Chef-Magic
7. Island Style Jamaican
8. Popie's Hotter 'n Hell
9. Pure Hell
10. Blazin' Saddle
11. Desert Rose Tango
12. San Francisco's
13. The Mean Green
14. Mezzetta California

15. Century Habañero
16. Esto Matara
17. Santa Fe Ole

Row 6
1. Popie's Original
2. Edun's Hot Pepper
3. Salu's Hot Reggae
4. Nel's Old Time Hot
5. Mayan Kut
6. Gibbons Louisiana
7. Brother Bru-Bru's
8. La Penca Salsa
9. Salsa de la Viuda
10. Grand Anse Obeah Oil
11. Amor
12. Tamazula Salsa
13. Salsa Huichol
14. Try Me Yucatan
15. Erica's Country Style
16. Chef Prudhomme's
17. Wing Club
18. Mosquito Coast
19. Road to Hell

Row 7
1. The Wizard
2. Brazos Beef
3. Pickapeppa
4. Bustelo's
5. Vic's Original
6. Hot Bitch
7. Green Isle
8. Trappey's Mexi
9. Clemente Jacques
10. Bello
11. Salu's
12. Montezuma Hab.
13. Gray's
14. Holy Habanero!
15. 911
16. Trappey's Red
17. Marie Sharp
18. Vernon's
19. Bueno
20. Tamarindo Bay

YELLOW POSTER

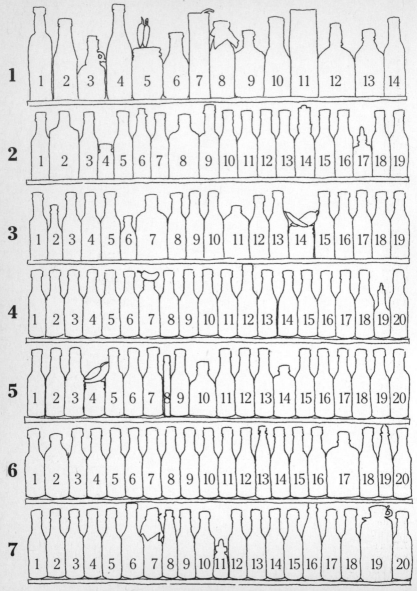

Key to Yellow Poster

These sauces are listed alphabetically in Section I.

Row 1
1. Dan T's
2. Caribbean Exotic
3. Tennessee Red
4. Eat This
5. Baptism of Fire
6. Johnny Wishbone
7. Texas Firecracker
8. Quest for Fire
9. Rasta Fire!
10. Wing-Time
11. Dave's Insanity
12. Kayak Jack
13. Halfway to Pure Hell
14. Golden Pacific

Row 2
1. The Brutal Bajan
2. Miss Anna's
3. KSOP
4. Redneck Gormay
5. Carib Islands
6. Lol-tun
7. Desert Pepper
8. Mango Creek
9. Waha Wera
10. Ted's Original
11. Dinosaur's Devils
12. Walker's Wood
13. Nor'Easter
14. Santa Sauce
15. Belligerant Blaze
16. Big Nose Kate
17. Fig's One Drop
18. Buckman's Best
19. Jo B's

Row 3
1. Dave's Hurtin'
2. Louisiana Crude
3. Southwest Spirit
4. Jamaican Gourmet
5. Marinda's
6. Petit Tabasco
7. Pain is Good
8. Wrong Number
9. Pa Chai Buffalo
10. Capt'n Sleepy's

Row 4
1. Tongues of Fire
2. Nali
3. Habanero Gold
4. Raging Inferno
5. Jump Up and Kiss Me
6. Fifi's Nasty Little Secret
7. Holy City Heat
8. Harrison's Atomic
9. Big John's Famous
10. Santa Fe Select
11. Mad Dog Inferno
12. Rosie Coyote's
13. Ultimate Burn
14. Ass in the Tub
15. Tropical Tastes
16. Crystal Classic
17. Tadpole's
18. Dixie Datil
19. Tabasco
20. Cape Fear

Row 5
1. Ass in Space
2. Atlanta Burning
3. Dallas Cowboy's
4. Eat This
5. Heat
6. Calido Chile Traders
7. Grenfruit
8. Doc McNeill's Final
9. Bad Girls in Heat
10. 99%
11. Hot Southern Nights
12. Tahiti Joe's
13. Hot Licks
14. Bubba Brand H'eatin
15. Smack My Ass

Row 1 (continued)
11. Asbirin
12. Justin Wllson's
13. River Run
14. Ralph's
15. A.S.C.
16. Kitten's Big Banana
17. Screamin' Demon
18. Hiccupin' Hot
19. Endorphin Rush

Row 6
1. Krista's Jamaican Hot
2. A Taste of Paradise
3. Mountainman
4. Satay
5. Anne and Steve's
6. The Brown Adobe
7. Captain Redbeard's
8. Cannon Ball
9. Grace Crushed Pepper
10. Endorphinator
11. Chipotle del Sol
12. Spicy Chesapeake
13. Axtexan
14. Mother's Mountain
15. Ozone Shooter
16. Dragon Fire
17. Pain is Good
18. Blair's Death Sauce
19. Diagnitas Aji
20. Prairie Fire

Row 7
1. Key West's
2. Jump Up and Kiss Me
3. Uncle Fred's 150K
4. Tropical Chile Co.
5. Gib's Nuclear Hell
6. Chief Trinidad
7. Georgia Peach
8. Tabasco Spice
9. Crawdad's Classics
10. Chile Today
11. Trauma Super
12. F.T. (no) Wimps
13. Swamp Island
14. Mean Devil Woman
15. Health Choice
16. Tennessee Bear's
17. Daytona Beach
18. Pearl's
19. not labeled
20. SLO JERK

Row (top-right)
16. Habañero with a Halflife
17. Chilli Peppers
18. Rass Mon
19. Gator Hammock
20. Castillo Salsa

ix

Section I is a listing of 551 hot sauces that appear in my three hot sauce posters or *The Great Hot Sauce Book*, and information about the folks who make sauces. Many are mom-and-pop operations, and addresses change — especially in the Caribbean after every hurricane. If you're a collector looking for a single bottle, many manufacturers will refer you to retail shops (see p. 52).

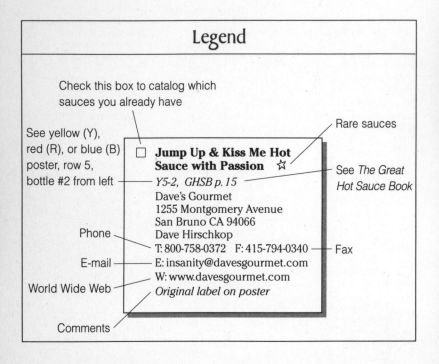

Legend

Check this box to catalog which sauces you already have

Rare sauces

See yellow (Y), red (R), or blue (B) poster, row 5, bottle #2 from left

☐ **Jump Up & Kiss Me Hot Sauce with Passion** ☆

Y5-2, GHSB p. 15

See *The Great Hot Sauce Book*

Dave's Gourmet
1255 Montgomery Avenue
San Bruno CA 94066
Dave Hirschkop

Phone

T: 800-758-0372   F: 415-794-0340

Fax

E-mail

E: insanity@davesgourmet.com

World Wide Web

W: www.davesgourmet.com

Original label on poster

Comments

I. Hot Sauce Manufacturers

☐ **A Taste of Paradise Caribbean Sunshine**

Y6-2, GHSB p. 3

A Taste of Paradise
P.O. Box 184, Cruz Bay
St. John, U.S. Virgin Islands 00831
Cheryl Miller
T: 809-776-6179   F: 809-776-6179

☐ **A.B. Hot Sauce** ☆

B5-8

Baumer Foods, Inc.
4301 Tulane Avenue
New Orleans, LA 70179-0166
Belinda Keasling
T: 504-482-5761   F: 504-483-2425
This sauce is rare in the U.S.; it's mostly exported.

☐ **A.S.C. "Reserved" Hot Sauce**

Y3-15

Adirondack Spice Company
P.O. Box 188
Eagle Bay, NY 13331-0188
T: 315-357-6247

☐ **ACME Almost Flammable Hot Sauce**

GHSB p. 48

Acme Bar & Grill
9 Great Jones Street
New York, NY 10012
T: 212-420-1934
This sauce comes in red or green, and is identical to El Yucateco.

☐ **Achiote Indian Sauce**

R1-10, GHSB p. 48

Hot Heads, Inc.
639 East Marion Street
Lancaster, PA 17602
Wendy Roda
T: 717-396-9784

☐ **Adobe Milling Jalapeño Hot Sauce**

B2-9, GHSB p. 48

Adobe Milling Company, Inc.
Box 596
Dove Creek, CO 81324
Ernest R. Waller
T: 800-542-3623   F: 970-677-2667

☐ **Adriatic Hot Ajvar**

GHSB p. 68

Importer: Jana Foods
22-11 38th Avenue
Long Island City, NY 11101
T: 718-482-9500   F: 718-482-9506

☐ **Aji Amazona Aji Verde en Vinagre**

GHSB p. 49

U.S. Fresh Marketing, Inc.
2304 Wake Forest Street
Virginia Beach, VA 23451
Tony Battaglia
T: 804-496-9300   F: 804-496-2733

☐ **Aji Amazona Salsa Roja Picante**

GHSB p. 49

U.S. Fresh Marketing, Inc.
See above

☐ **America's Cup '95** ☆

GHSB p. 49
Keeler Kommunications
Andrew Keeler
T: 415-865-0191   F: 415-865-0192
E: andrew@keelerkom.com
*Made for the America's
Cup; Andrew has a few bottles left.*

☐ **Amor**

R6-11
Mexican Spice and Food Co.
P.O. Box 83956,
San Diego, CA, 92138
Toly Monge
T: 619-279-3221   F: 619-279-3247

☐ **Ana Belly Extra Salsa Picante**

B4-2, GHSB p. 50
Alimentos Y Conservas Ana
   Belly, S.A.
Guatemala

☐ **Andre's Rouge Spiced Cajun
Hot Sauce**

B5-15, GHSB p. 36
All Cajun Food Company
1019 Delcambre Road
Breaux Bridge, LA 70517
Bruci Gauthier
T: 800-467-3613   F: 318-332-1467
*This sauce's original label is on the
blue poster; the new label is in the
book.*

☐ **Andy's Good 'n Hot Stuff**

B1-11
Andy's Good 'n Hot Stuff
P.O. Box 284
D'Lo, MS, 39062
Billie Burkhart
T: 800-HOT-4399

☐ **Anne and Steve's Love
Potion #1**

Y6-5
Sgt. Pepper's Hot Sauce
   Micro Brewery
Box 49565
Austin, TX 78765
J. P. Hayes
T: 512-371-7727
*This sauce was made for a friend's
wedding.*

☐ **Another Bloody Day
in Paradise**

B2-13, GHSB p. 36
Peppers
2009 Highway One
Dewey Beach, DE 19971
Chip Hearn
T: 800-998-FIRE   F: 302 227 4603
E: peppers@peppers.com
W: peppers.com

☐ **Arizona Gunslinger**

B7-9, GHSB p. 50
Arizona Pepper Products Co.
P.O. Box 40605
Mesa, AZ 85274
Dan Eggen
T: 602-833-1908   F: 602-464-2077

☐ **Asbirin Hot Sauce**

Y3-11

Fig Tree Food Distributors
239 North Causeway Boulevard
Metairie, LA 70001
Tony Nelson
T: 800-886-6354 F: 504-524-8941
W: gourmail@earthlink.com

☐ **Ass Kickin' Hot Sauce**

B3-15, GHSB p. 50

Southwest Specialty Food Co.
5805 West McLellan #3
Glendale, AZ 85301
Jeff Jacobs
T: 602-931-3131 F: 602-931-9931

☐ **Ass in Space Hot Sauce**

Y5-1

Fig Tree Food Distributors
See Asbirin Hot Sauce, p. 3

☐ **Ass in the Tub Hot Sauce**

Y4-14

Fig Tree Food Distributors
See Asbirin Hot Sauce, p. 3

☐ **Atlanta Burning Hot Sauce**

GHSB p. 78

Redwine Farms
3781 Happy Valley Circle
Newnan, GA 30263
Bob Witt
T: 404-253-8100

☐ **Atlanta Burning Super Hot Sauce**

Y5-2

Redwine Farms
See above

☐ **Ayla's Organics Red Pepper Sauce**

R1-11

Spectrum Naturals
133 Copeland Street
Petaluma, CA 94952

☐ **Aztexan Pepper Company Habañero Supreme Hot Sauce**

Y6-13, GHSB p. 51

Aztexan Pepper Co.
P.O. Box 1032
Austin, TX 78767
Mark Witt
T: 512-448-9660 F: 512-448-9660
The sauce's original label is in the book; the new label is on the poster.

☐ **Bad Girls in Heat**

Y5-9

PepperTown
7561 Woodman Place
Van Nuys, CA 91405
T: 800-973-7738

☐ **Bandana's Serious Habañero Pepper Sauce**

B5-3

Bandana's Serious Pepper Products
P.O. Box 110
St. Peters, PA 19470
Susan and Ted Dames
T: 610-286-7986
E: bandan@fast.net
W: pages.prodigy.com/bandana

☐ **Bandana's XXtra Serious Habañero Pepper Sauce**

GHSB p. 3

See above

3

☐ **Baptism of Fire**

Y1-5
Pata Inc.
RR 2 Box 71
Hubbard, TX 76648
T: 817-576-2154 F: 817-576-2870

☐ **Barbados Jack Island Hot Sauce**

B4-18
L. G. Miller & Sons Ltd.
Wildey, Barbados
Patricia McLean
T: 809-427-4310 F: 809-429-2736

☐ **Baron West Indian Hot Sauce**

R4-14
Baron Foods Ltd., c/o Russo & Assoc.
P.O. Box 4746
Foster City, CA 94404
Christina Russo
T: 415-574-6948 F: 415-345-0535

☐ **Bat's Brew**

B5-4, GHSB p. 78
Panola Pepper Corporation
Route 2, Box 148
Lake Providence, LA 71254
Grady Brown
T: 800-256-3013 F: 318-559-3003

☐ **Batten Island**

R2-15, GHSB p. 78
M&W of Jax
P.O. Box 8667
Jacksonville, FL 32239
Marcus Rawls
T: 800-335-7880 F: 904-757-6100

☐ **Belligerent Blaze**

Y2-15
El's Fire Sauce
909 72nd Street North
St. Petersburg, FL 33710
J. Loren
T: 813-344-FIRE

☐ **Bello Hot Pepper Sauce**

R7-10
Parry W. Bellot & Co., Ltd.
Castle Comfort, P.O. Box 22
Roseau, Dominica, West Indies
Irene Esch
T: 809-448-2860 F: 809-448-2053

☐ **Berrak Aci Biber Sosu**

GHSB p. 68
Berrak, Zeytursan AS
Turkey
T: 212-615-6603 F: 212-563-0886

☐ **Big John's Famous Key West Hot Sauce**

GHSB p. 4
Jones Productions
Box 362
Key West, FL 33041
Trish Jones
T: 305-296-1863

☐ **Big John's Famous Key West Mango Fandango Hot Sauce**

Y4-9
Jones Productions
See above

4

☐ **Big John's Key West Really, Really Hot Sauce**

GHSB p. 4
Jones Productions
See above

☐ **Big Nose Kate's Habañero Sauce**

Y2-16
Big Nose Kate's Saloon
P.O. Box 357
Tombstone, AZ 85638
Gloria Goldstein
T: 520-457-3405   F: 520-457-3405

☐ **Bill Wharton's Liquid Summer**

B2-7, GHSB p. 79
Wharton Pepper Company
Route 3 Box 124-L
Monticello, FL 32344
Bill Wharton
T: 904-997-4359

☐ **Blair's After Death Sauce**

GHSB p. 115
Gardner Resources
P.O. Box 363
Highlands, NJ 07732
Blair Lazar
T: 800-98BLAIR   F: 908-291-3605
E: BLAIR30@aol.com

☐ **Blair's Death Sauce**

Y6-18, GHSB p. 96
Gardner Resources
See above

☐ **Blazin' Saddle**

R5-10, GHSB p. 4
Jardine's Texas Foods
Jardine Ranch
Buda, TX 78610
T: 800-544-1880   F: 512-295-3020

☐ **Bob Harris Hot Ideas Hot Sauce**

GHSB p. 56
Hot Sauce Harry's
3422 Flair Drive
Dallas, TX 75229
Bob & Dianne Harris
T: 214-902-8552   F: 214-956-9885
E: freecatalog@hotsauceharrys.com
W: hotsauceharrys.com

☐ **Bone Suckin' Sauce**

GHSB p. 79
Ford's Foods, Inc.
1109 Agriculture Street
Raleigh, NC 27603
Sandi Ford
T: 800-446-0947   F: 919-821-5781

☐ **Bonney Pepper Sauce**

R3-4, GHSB p. 4
Westlow's
West Indies Trading Company
6841 Louis XIV Street
New Orleans, LA 70124
Elizabeth Odom
T: 504-837-2766

☐ **Bourbon Street Fire Sauce**
R4-3, GHSB p. 79
Bourbon Street Grill
213 College Street
Burlington, VT 05402
Arthur O'Connor
T: 800-736-5593   F: 802-658-2038

☐ **Bowman's Hot Pepper
Sauce** ☆
R1-5
Bowman's
St. Vincent, West Indies
T: 809-457-1026

☐ **Brazos Beef Emporium
Cowboy Cayenne Pepper
Sauce**
R7-2, GHSB p. 51
Brazos Country Foods
700 South Bryan Street
Bryan, TX 77803-3928
Craig Conlee
T: 409-775-1611   F: 409-775-1917

☐ **Brother Bru-Bru's African
Hot Sauce**
R6-7, GHSB p. 68
Brother Bru Bru
P.O. Box 2964
Venice, CA 90291
Bruce Langhorne
T: 310-396-9033   F: 310-396-9033

☐ **Brother Bru-Bru's Mild
African Hot Sauce**
GHSB p. 68
Brother Bru Bru
See above

☐ **Bubba Brand H'eatin
Hot Sauce**
Y5-14, GHSB p. 80
Atlantis Coastal Foods, Inc.
708 King Street
Charleston, SC 29403
Wesley Fredsell
T: 803-853-9444   F: 803-853-8463

☐ **Buckman's Best Habañero
(Below Hell) Hot Sauce**
Y2-18
Lendy's
1581 General Booth Blvd., Suite 101
Virginia Beach, VA 23454
Bob Buckman
T: 757-491-3511   F: 757-491-8821

☐ **Bueno Pickled Piquin Peppers**
R7-18
Bueno Foods
2001 4th Street SW
Albuquerque, NM 87102
Sue Phillips
T: 800-888-7336

☐ **Bufalo Jalapeño Mexican
Hot Sauce**
B1-8
Monterrey Food Products
3939 Cesar Chavez Avenue
Los Angeles, CA 90063-1899
Peter X. Galindo, Jr.
T: 213-263-2143   F: 213-263-2545

☐ **Busha Browne's Pukka Hot Pepper Sauce**

B6-8, GHSB p. 5

Busha Browne Company Ltd.
  (c/o Infood)
135 County Road
Cresskill, NJ 07626
Sara Stern
T: 201-569-3175

☐ **Busha Browne's Spicy & Hot Pepper Sherry Sauce**

GHSB p. 5

Busha Browne Company Ltd.
See above

☐ **Busha Browne's Spicy Jerk Sauce**

R2-4, GHSB p. 5

Busha Browne Company Ltd.
See above

☐ **Bustelo's Chipotle Pepper Sauce**

GHSB p. 52

Bustelo's Backyard
P.O. Box 231
Occidental, CA 95465
Larry Watson
T: 707-874-1663

☐ **Bustelo's Habañero Pepper Sauce**

GHSB p. 80

Bustelo's Backyard
See above

☐ **Bustelo's Very Hot Pepper Sauce**

R7-4, GHSB p. 80

Bustelo's Backyard
See above

☐ **Cafe Louisiane Hotter'n Hell Sauce**

GHSB p. 36

Garden Row Foods, Inc.
905 North California Avenue
Chicago, IL 60622
George Kosten
T: 800-223-3495
Cafe Louisiane was purchased by Garden Row.

☐ **Cajun Rush Hot Pepper Sauce**

R3-17

Cajun Rush
22295 Gull Street
Maurepas, LA 70449
Rush Biossat
T: 504-695-6692

☐ **Cajun Rush XXX Hot Pepper Sauce**

GHSB p. 37

Cajun Rush
See above

☐ **Calido Chile Traders Besos de Fuego**

Y5-6, GHSB p. 81

Calido Chile Traders
5360 Merriam Drive
Merriam, KS 66203
R.J. Samuels
T: 800-LUTTHOT F: 816-931-6779

☐ **California Perfect Pepper Sauce**

R1-9, GHSB p. 81
Santa Barbara Creative Foods
32 West Anapamu Street #115
Santa Barbara, CA 93101
Jenny Ballestrin
T: 800-735-1565 F: 805-566-9380

☐ **Candido Piri Piri**

GHSB p. 69
ETS Candido
34 Rue Benoit Frachon
Champignysurmarne, France

☐ **Cannon Ball Hot Sauce**

Y6-8
Flamingo Flats
406 Talbot Street
St. Michael's, MD 21663
Bob Deppe
T: 800-HOT-8841

☐ **Cape Fear Hot Sauce**

Y4-20
Thunder Bay
126 Chowan Drive
Portsmouth, VA 23701
T: 757-465-7235 F: 757-465-7237

☐ **Capital Punishment**

B4-11, GHSB p. 108
Hot Heads, Inc.
See Achiote Indian Sauce, p. 1

☐ **Capt'n Sleepy's Habañero Hot Sauce**

Y3-10
Capt'n Sleepy Enterprises, Inc.
6526 Peacock Road
Siesta Key, FL 34242

☐ **Captain Redbeard's Habañero Pepper Sauce**

GHSB p. 5
Captain Foods, Inc.
2220 Hibiscus Drive, Suite 4
Edgewater, FL 32141
Douglas D. Feindt
T: 800-749-5047 F: 904-428-5833

☐ **Captain Redbeard's Olde Florida Hot Sauce**

GHSB p. 81
Captain Foods, Inc.
See above

☐ **Captain Redbeard's Sharkbite Habañero Pepper Sauce**

Y6-7
Captain Foods, Inc.
See above

☐ **Carib Islands Bucco Reef Island Hot Sauce**

Y2-5
Carib Islands Trading Company
1991 Corporate Square #179
Longwood, FL 32750
Karen Hulbert
T: 800-919-9195 F: 407-339-1111

☐ **Caribbean Exotic Gourmet Hot Sauce**

Y1-2
Atlantic International Traders
P.O. Box 113005
Miami, FL 33111-3005
T: 305-372-9547 F: 305-381-6527

☐ **Caribbee Pepper Sauce**

R3-6
Sunny Caribbee Spice Company
P.O. Box 3237 V.D.A.
St.Thomas, U.S. Virgin Islands 0803
Greg Gunter
T: 809-494-2178   F: 809-494-4039

☐ **Caribe Cookery Bajan
Hot Sauce**

B5-6
Caribe Cookery
*I was unable to locate this
company; they are from Barbados.*

☐ **Casa Fiesta**

B7-6, GHSB p. 37
Bruce Foods Corporation
Drawer 1030
New Iberia, LA 70561
Virginia Brown
T: 318-365-8101   F: 318-364-3742

☐ **Castillo Salsa Habañero**

Y5-20, GHSB p. 52
Especiales Castillo S.A. de C.V.
Asteroides Y Satelites # 7, Parque
   Industrial
Apt. P.O.stal 2-45, CP 83290
Hermosillo, Mexico
T: 62-51-00-58   F: 62-51-08-58

☐ **Century Habañero Pepper
Sauce**

GHSB p. 82
Century Sauce Kitchens
Box 4057
Copley, OH 44321
Kathleen Redle
T: 800-831-4687   F: 330-666-2578

☐ **Century Hot Pepper Sauce**

R5-15
Century Sauce Kitchens
See above

☐ **Chef Hans' Jalapeño
Hot Sauce**

B2-14
Chef Hans Gourmet Foods
Box 3252
Monroe, LA 71210
Chef Hans
T: 800-256-4267   F: 318-322-2340

☐ **Chef Hans' Louisiana
Hot Sauce**

GHSB p. 37
Chef Hans Gourmet Foods
See above

☐ **Chef Paul Prudhomme's
Magic Pepper Sauce**

R6-16, GHSB p. 38
Chef Paul Prudhomme's
824 Distributor's Row, P.O. Box 23342
Harahan, LA 70183-0342
John L. McBride
T: 800-457-2857   F: 504-731-3576

☐ **Chesapeake Bay Habañero
Hot Sauce**

Y6-12, GHSB p. 82
Chesapeake Bay Habañero Hot
   Sauce Co.
5737 Craneybrook Lane
Portsmouth, VA 23703
Matthew Cobb
T: 800-655-9132

9

☐ **Chesapeake Baybe**
McNeill Inc.
2855 West Oakland Drive
Wilmington, DE 19808
Susan McNeill
T: 302-996-9054   F: 302-996-0231
W: heatmeup.com

☐ **Chief Trinidad Hot Sauce**
R1-4
Chief Brand Products
Uriah Butler Highway
Charlieville, Chaguanas, Trinidad,
   West Indies
Shaieb Khan
T: 809-665-4144   F: 809-665-5006

☐ **Chief Trinidad Hot Sauce**
Y7-6, GHSB p. 6
Chief Brand Products
See above

☐ **Chile Today Hot Tamale
Smoked Habañero Sauce**
Y7-10, GHSB p. 82
Chile Today Hot Tamale
919 Highway 33, Suite 47
Freehold, NJ 07728
Rob Polishook
T: 800-468-7377   F: 908-308-1717

☐ **Chilli Peppers Hot Sauce**
Y5-17
Chilli Peppers Restaurant
3001 North Croatan Highway
Kill Devil Hills, NC 27948
T: 919-441-8081   F: 919-480-HOTA

☐ **Chipotle Del Sol Smokin'
Hot Sauce**
Y6-11
Sgt. Pepper's Hot Sauce Micro
   Brewery
See Anne and Steve's Love Potion
   #1, p. 2

☐ **Cholimex Chilli Sauce**
R1-8
Cholimex
*I was unable to locate this
company.*

☐ **Cholula Hot Sauce**
B2-10, GHSB p. 52
Jalisco Food Company
16414 San Pedro, Suite 900
San Antonio, TX 78232
T: 210-495-2995   F: 210-495-2740

☐ **Chombo Sauce**
R4-10
D'Elidas
Intermerica Trade Company
Monroe, TX 77301

☐ **Clancy's Fancy**
B2-4, GHSB p. 83
Clancy's Fancy
410 West Washington
Ann Arbor, MI 48103
C. Richard Raynor
T: 313-663-4338

☐ **Clemente Jacques**
R7-9
Clemente Jacques
SA de CV
Queretaro, Mexico

10

☐ **Cosmopolitan Sambal Wayang Bawang Putih**

GHSB p. 69
Cosmopolitan Foods
138 Essex Avenue
Glen Ridge, NJ 07028
Nick Ten Velde
T: 201-680-4560   F: 201-743-4790

☐ **Cosmopolitan Sambal Wayang Kerrie**

GHSB p. 69
Cosmopolitan Foods
See above

☐ **Country Home Hot Pepper Sauce**

GHSB p. 6
RAJ Imports
21822 Ospery Lane
Moreno Valley, CA 92557
Richard Johnson
T: 909-369-8647

☐ **Coyote Cocina Howlin' Hot Sauce**

B4-10, GHSB p. 112
Coyote Cocina
1364 Rufina Circle #1
Santa Fe, NM 87501
Tina Jo Paul
T: 800-866-HOWL   F: 505-989-9026
W: santa-fe-style-foods.com/
Coyote.html

☐ **Coyote Cocina Smoky Chipotle Sauce**

B2-1, GHSB p. 53
Coyote Cocina
See above

☐ **Coyote Cocina Tangy Taco Sauce**

GHSB p. 53
Coyote Cocina
See above

☐ **Craig's HOT! Pepper Sauce**

B5-9, GHSB p. 112
Capsico Foods, Inc.
18 South Avenue West, Suite 180
Cranford, NJ 07016
Craig Neivert
T: 908-272-8687   F: 201-939-5112

☐ **Crawdad's Classics Hot Sauce**

YR7-9
Crawdad's Classics Gourmet
3351 West Birchwood
Springfield, MO 65807
Cordell Bixler
T: 417-886-2564   F: 417-886-2564

☐ **Crazy Cajun Piquante Sauce**

B2-18
Crazy Cajun Enterprises
P.O. Box 804
Cobb, CA 95246
Charley Addison
T: 707-928-4392   F: 707-928-4365

☐ **Creative Chef Hot Peppered Orange Sauce**

GHSB p. 83
The Creative Chef
20125 South Pickering Road
Belton, MO 64012
Fred Fatino
T: 816-322-3248   F: 816-331-8171

☐ **Creole "Shut My Mouth" Pepper Sauce**
B1-4
Maison Louisianne, LA

☐ **Crystal Classic Habañero Sauce**
Y4-16
Baumer Foods, Inc.
See A.B. Hot Sauce, p. 1

☐ **Crystal Extra Hot Hot Sauce**
GHSB p. 38
Baumer Foods, Inc.
See A.B. Hot Sauce, p. 1

☐ **Crystal Hot Sauce**
B7-4, GHSB p. 38
Baumer Foods, Inc.
See A.B. Hot Sauce, p. 1
Note the Arabic lettering.

☐ **Dallas Cowboy's Hot Sauce**
Y5-3
Hot Sauce Harry's
See Bob Harris Hot Ideas Hot Sauce, p. 5

☐ **Dan T's Inferno Mustard Cayenne Sauce**
GHSB p. 101
Dan T's Inferno Foods Ltd.
1-216 Queen Street South Streetsville
Mississauga, Ontario, Canada, L5M1L5
Theresa Taylor
T: 905-858-7593

☐ **Dan T's Inferno Spiced Cayenne Sauce**
GHSB p. 101
Dan T's Inferno Food's Ltd.
See above

☐ **Dan T's Inferno Whitehot Cayenne Sauce**
Y1-1, GHSB p. 101
Dan T's Inferno Foods Ltd.
See above

☐ **Dat'l Do-It Hot Sauce**
GHSB p. 6
Dat'l Do-It Shop
3255 Parker Drive
St. Augustine, FL 32095
Christopher Way
T: 800-468-3285   F: 904-829-9191

☐ **Dave's Hurtin' Habañero Sauce**
Y3-1
Dave's Gourmet
1255 Montgomery Avenue
San Bruno CA 94066
Dave Hirschkop
T: 800-758-0372   F: 415-794-0340
E: insanity@davesgourmet.com
W: davesgourmet.com

☐ **Dave's Insanity Private Reserve, Limited Edition**
Y1-11, GHSB p. 115
Dave's Gourmet
See above

Dave's Insanity Sauce
BR2-9, GHSB p. 115
Dave's Gourmet
See above

**Dave's Insanity Sauce II:
The Second Burning**
GHSB p. 83
Dave's Gourmet
See above
The original label is shown.

**Dave's Temporary
Insanity Sausa**
R2-5
Dave's Gourmet
See above
The original label is shown.

**Daytona Beach Bike Week
'96 Hot Sauce**
Y7-17, GHSB p. 53
Captain Foods, Inc.
See Captain Redbeard's Habañero
   Pepper Sauce, p. 8

Desert Fire Hot Sauce
B3-18, GHSB p. 53
Southwest Specialty Food Co.
See Ass Kickin' Hot Sauce, p. 3

**Desert Pepper XXX
Habañero Pepper Sauce**
Y2-7
El Paso Chile Company
909 Texas Avenue
El Paso TX 79901
Jim Baker
T: 800-274-7468   F: 915-544-7552

**Desert Rose Tamarind
Hot Sauce**
GHSB p. 84
Desert Rose Foods, Inc.
P.O. Box 5391
Tucson, AZ 85703
Mary Schaheen
T: 800-937-2572   F: 520-620-0406
W: biz.rtd.com/desert_rose

**Desert Rose Tango Papaya
Hot Sauce**
R5-11
Desert Rose Foods Inc.
See above

Devil Drops
B6-1, GHSB p. 6
Dat'l Do-It Shop
See Dat'l Do-It Hot Sauce, p. 12

Dewey Beach Fire
B6-2, GHSB p. 39
Peppers
See Another Bloody Day in
   Paradise, p. 2

Diaguitas Aji
Y6-19, GHSB p. 54
Embarcadero Home Cannery
2026 Livingston Street
Oakland, CA 94606
Louis Nagel
T: 510-535-2311   F: 510-535-2235

☐ Dilijan Liquid Spice

B4-5, GHSB p. 69
Dilijan Products
P.O. Box 145
Ringoes, NJ 08551-0145
Steven C. Kachigian
T: 800-368-9223   F: 908-788-6989

☐ Dinosaur's Devils Duel

Y2-11, GHSB p. 101
Dinosaur Bar B Que
246 West Willow Street
Syracuse, NY 13202
John or Mike
T: 315-476-4937

☐ Dixie Datil Pepper Sauce

Y4-18
Thom-Kat Enterprises
5325 Porter Road Extension
St. Augustine, FL 32095
T: 800-81D-IXIE

☐ Doc McNeill's Final Experiment (test tube)

Y5-8
McNeill Inc.
See Chesapeake Baybe, p. 10

☐ Don Alfonso Chipotles en Adobo

B2-3
Don Alfonso Foods
P.O. Box 201988
Austin, TX 78720-1988
Jose Marmolejo
T: 512-335-2370   F: 512-335-0636

☐ Dr. J's Habañero Chile Elixir

B6-9, GHSB p. 54
Dr. J's Kitchen, Inc.
702 Coronado Rd.
Corrales, NM 87048
Jerry V. Mayeux
T: 505-898-6700   F: 505-898-7895

☐ Dragon Fire

Y6-16
South Side Pepper Company
320 North Walnut Street
Mechanicsburg, PA 17055
T: 717-691-7132   F: 717-691-8684

☐ Ducal Hot Sauce ☆

GHSB p. 54
Alimentos Kern de Guatemala
KM 6½ Karatira Al Atlantico
Guatemala

☐ Durkee RedHot Cayenne Pepper Sauce

B3-3
Reckitt & Colman
1655 Valley Road, Box 943
Wayne, NJ 07474-0943
T: 201-633-2603   F: 201-633-3633

☐ E.M.G. Local Pepper Sauce ☆

R1-1
E.M.G.
St. Vincent, West Indies
T: 809-458-4191
I found this sauce at a roadside stand.

☐ **Eat This "Soul Sauce"**

Y5-4
Eat This, Inc.
P.O. Box 2474
Breckenridge, CO 80424

☐ **Eat This Strawberry
Habañero Soul Sauce**

Y1-4
Eat This, Inc.
See above

☐ **Edun's Caribbean
Pepper Sauce**

GHSB p. 7
Edun's Homemade Preserves
P.O. Box 3122
Carolina, PR 00984-3122
Wendy-Lisa Carter
T: 809-769-6138

☐ **Edun's Hot Pepper Sauce** ☆

R6-2
Edun's Homemade Preserves
See above

☐ **El Gallero Salsa Picante** ☆

GHSB p. 55
Raul Chavez Cuervo
Litoral 2909 S.J.
Guadalajara, Mexico 101517

☐ **El Yucateco**

B3-13, GHSB p. 55
Priamo J. Gamboa O.
Calle 32 No 506-0, por 63465
Merida, Yucatan, Mexico
Priamo Jose Gamboa
*El Yucateco comes in red and
green.*

☐ **Endorphin Rush**

Y3-19, GHSB p. 116
Garden Row Foods, Inc.
See Cafe Louisiane Hotter'n Hell
   Sauce, p. 7

☐ **Endorphinator Mango
BBQ Sauce**

Y6-10, GHSB p. 55
Jeffrey's Restaurant
1204 West Lynn Street
Austin, TX 78703
David Garrido
T: 512-477-5584

☐ **Erica's Country Style
Pepper Sauce**

R6-15, GHSB p. 7
Erica's Country Style Products
Box 748
St. Vincent, West Indies
Erica McIntosh

☐ **Eslat Wheat Germ** ☆

GHSB p. 84
Eslat (Caribbean Limited)
20 Farfan Street
Arema, Trinidad, West Indies
T: 809-667-0493

☐ **Esto Matara Los Gringos
New Year 1994**

R5-16
Bustelo's Backyard
See Bustelo's Chipotle Pepper
   Sauce, p. 7

☐ **Evadney's All-Purpose Jamaican Hot Sauce**
B1-3, GHSB p. 8
Island Imports, Inc.
P.O. Box 78925
Los Angeles, CA 90016
Francis W. Hamilton

☐ **Evadney's Fire Water Hot Sauce**
B5-14, GHSB p. 7
Island Imports, Inc.
See above

☐ **Evadney's Habañero Pickled Pepper Sauce**
R3-9
Island Imports, Inc.
See above

☐ **Eve's Pepper Sauce** ☆
GHSB p. 8
Milford Road, Shirvan
Tobago
Yvonne Williams

☐ **Fifi's Nasty Little Secret**
Y4-6
PepperTown
See Bad Girls in Heat, p. 3

☐ **Fig's One Drop Hot Sauce**
Y2-17
Fig Tree Food Distributors
See Asbirin Hot Sauce, p. 3

☐ **Fire in the Hole Habañero Hot Sauce**
GHSB p. 56
Brazos Country Foods
See Brazos Beef Emporium, p. 6

☐ **Firehouse Global Warming**
GHSB p. 96
Firehouse Bar & Grill
1525 Blake Street
Denver, CO 80202
Derrick Nickel
T: 303-820-3308   F: 303-446-3060

☐ **Firehouse Satan's Slow Burn**
GHSB p. 102
Firehouse Bar & Grill
See above

☐ **Fire in the Hole Habañero Hot Sauce**
GHSB p. 56
Brazos Country Foods
See Brazos Beef Emporium, p. 6

☐ **Firemist Spray Hot Sauce**
GHSB p. 85
EDS Erickson Development
13642 Laraway Drive
Riverview, FL 33569
Michael Erickson

☐ **Firey Louisiana Hot Sauce**
B2-5
Baumer Foods, Inc.
See A.B. Hot Sauce, p. 1

Fish Camp Habañero Sauce ☆

B6-18. GHSB p. 56
Jeffrey's Restaurant
See Endorphinator Mango BBQ
    Sauce, p. 15

Flaming Yellow Canary

GHSB p. 85
Rick's Kitchen
P.O. Box 1702
Cashiers, NC 28717
Rick Brooks
T: 704-743-2272

Flam-n-John

R4-11
Hot Heads, Inc.
See Achiote Indian Sauce, p. 1

Flame Louisiana Hot Sauce

B4-8
Baumer Foods, Inc.
See A.B. Hot Sauce, p. 1

Flying Burrito Flounder Juice

B7-5, GHSB p. 85
Flying Burrito
746 Airport Road
Chapel Hill, NC, 27514
Vicki Campbell
T: 919-967-7744

Forbes Ground Red Peppers

GHSB p. 8
M. Forbes Company
Brooklyn, NY 11212

Fort Worth Flame

GHSB p. 56
Hot Sauce Harry's
See Bob Harris Hot Ideas Hot
    Sauce, p. 5

Freddy's Big Boy's Hot Sauce

R2-10
Homemade by a friend's daughter.

F.T. (no) Wimps

Y7-12, GHSB p. 84
Rick's Kitchen
See Flaming Yellow Canary, p. 17

Gator Hammock Gator Sauce

R1-16
Gator Hammock
Highway 29
Felda, FL 33930
Buddy Taylor
T: 800-66-GATOR
E: hotgator@iline.com
W: iline.com/hotgator/hotgator.htm

Gator Hammock Swamp Mustard

Y5-19
Gator Hammock
See above

Gecko Exxxtra Hot Jalapeño Salsa Verde ☆

B1-9
Gecko Fun Foods
Box 39036
San Antonio, TX 78218
Robert Jennings
T: 210-822-7122
This sauce has been discontinued.

17

☐ **Georgia Peach and Vidalia Onion Hot Sauce**

Y7-7

Peppers
See Another Bloody Day in
    Paradise, p. 2

☐ **Gibbons Louisiana Salsa Picante**

R6-6, GHSB p. 39

J.T. Gibbons, Inc.
New Orleans, LA 70179

☐ **Gib's Mo' Hotter Bottled Hell**

R1-13

Gib's Classics, Inc.
P.O. Box 5278
Louisville, KY 40255-0278
Ray Gibson
T: 800-881-5233   F: 502-473-7214

☐ **Gib's Nuclear Hell Hot Pepper Sauce**

Y7-5, GHSB p. 96

Gib's Classics, Inc.
See above

☐ **Golden Pacific Island Honey Chili Sauce**

Y1-14

Golden Pacific Island Foods
P.O. Box 1986, Suite 381
Morgan Hill, CA 95038
Jeffrey Marcil
T: 800-648-8439   F: 408-776-1096

☐ **Goldwin Garlic Chilli Sauce** ☆

GHSB p. 70

Wee Seng Hng Trading
94-B, Jalan Senang, Singapore 1441

☐ **Goya Hot Sauce**

R2-11, GHSB p. 40

Goya Foods
100 Seaview Drive
Secaucus, NJ 07094

☐ **Grace Crushed Pepper Sauce, Y, 6-9**

Grace Foods
3714 Birchwood Court
North Brunswick, NJ 08902
Derrick Reckord
T: 908-840-4007   F: 908-840-4087

☐ **Grace Original Jamaican Hot Pepper Sauce**

R3-14

Grace Foods
See above

☐ **Grand Anse #5**

R4-13

H.A. Reis
P.O. Box 6280
St. Thomas, U.S. Virgin Islands
    00804-6280
Sebastiano Paiewonsky
T: 800-524-2037   F: 809-777-1616

☐ **Grand Anse Island Jerk! Grill Sauce**

GHSB p. 9

H.A. Reis
See above

☐ **Grand Anse Moki Moki Mustard Sauce**

GHSB p. 9

H.A. Reis
See above

18

☐ **Grand Anse Moko Jumbie**

B6-6, GHSB p. 9
H.A. Reis
See above

☐ **Grand Anse Obeah Oil**

R6-10
H.A. Reis
See above

☐ **Grand Anse Peppa-Po**

R5-5
H.A. Reis
See above

☐ **Gray's Hot Pepper Sauce**

R7-13, GHSB p. 9
Excelsior Trading Co., Inc.
7980 NW 67th Street
Miami, FL 33166
Raymond Chai-Chang
T: 305-594-1142   F: 305-594-0274

☐ **Green Isle Pepper Sauce**

R7-7
Parry W. Bellot & Co., Ltd.
See Bello Hot Pepper Sauce, p. 4

☐ **Grenfruit Hot Sauce**

Y5-7, GHSB p. 9
Grenfruit Woman's Cooperative
Grand Roy, St. Johns
Grenada, West Indies
Leslie Ann Mark
T: 809-444-8894
Imported by C. Russo, P.O. Box
   4746, Foster City, CA 94404

☐ **Grenfruit Spicy Sauce**

GHSB p. 9
Grenfruit Woman's Cooperative
See above

☐ **Gunsam's Hot Sauce** ☆

R1-12, GHSB p. 10
L. Gunsam & Son
Kingston
St. Vincent, West Indies
T: 71125
Imported by Baron Foods LTD
   (See Baron, p. 4)

☐ **HP Chilli Sauce**

R1-2
I found this in Great Britain —
no address.

☐ **Habañero !HOT! !HOT! !HOT!**

R4-18, GHSB p. 10
Thalcash Network
11409 East Evans Avenue
Aurora, CO 80014
Alois P. Dogue
T: 303-750-2150

☐ **Habañero Gold**

Y4-3
Habañero Gold
162 Claflin Boulevard
Franklin Square, NY 11010
Lorraine Madaffari
T: 516-328-0781
E: HabneroGld@aol.com

☐ **Habañero Hot Sauce from Hell**
B7-11, GHSB p. 102
Southwest Specialty Food Co.
See Ass Kickin' Hot Sauce, p. 3
*Bottles with red dripping wax cap
are now rare.*

☐ **Habañero Hot Sauce with a
Half Life**
Y5-16, GHSB p. 97
Wild Bill Hickory, Inc.
9800 Martin Road
Clarence Center, NY 14032
Bill Richer
T: 716-741-8234   F: 716-741-8234
E: wildbill@buffnet.net
W: buffnet.net/~wildbill/

☐ **Halfway to Pure Hell
Hot Sauce**
Y1-13, GHSB p. 102
Two Chefs
Box 101684
Denver, CO 80250
Eric Walton
T: 800-PURHELL

☐ **Harissa**
B6-7
Good Eats Company
65 East Washington Avenue
Washington, NJ 07882
Sim Baron
T: 908-689-4655   F: 908-689-4813

☐ **Harissa Dea**
B6-7, GHSB p. 70
Otra Barbier Dauphin
BP 45 13151 Tarascon
France

☐ **Harissa Le Flambeau du
Cap Bon**
GHSB p. 70
Socona, B. P. 93
1015 Tunisia R. P.

☐ **Harrison's Atomic Hot Sauce**
Y4-8
Harrison's Food Products
403 Atlantic Blvd
Atlantic Beach, FL 32233
Ben Davidowitz
T: 904-246-0056   F: 904-241-5788
E: hogendog@jaxnet.com
W: ipcc.com/market/boulevard

☐ **Hawaiian Passion Fire Sauce**
B6-4, GHSB p. 86
Hawaiian Plantations
53-086 Halai Road
Hau'ula, HI 96717
Chris Johnson
T: 808-293-8233   F: 808-293-8233

☐ **Hawaiian Passion Lilikoi
Hot Sauce**
GHSB p. 86
Hawaiian Plantations
See above

☐ **Hawaiian Passion Pineapple
Pepper Sauce**
B3-17, GHSB p. 86
Hawaiian Plantations
See above

☐ **Health Choice Dam' Hot Pepper Sauce**

Y7-15
Tropical Temptations, Inc.
P.O. Box 9746
Fort Lauderdale, FL 33310
David Reed
T: 800-743-2793   F: 800-743-2798
E: david@4tropical.com
W: 4tropical.com

☐ **Heat**

Y5-5, GHSB p. 86
Rick's Kitchen
See Flaming Yellow Canary, p. 17

☐ **Heatwave North Side Hot Sauce**

B5-11, GHSB p. 10
North Side Hot Sauce
Box 5564
St.Thomas, U.S. Virgin Islands 00803
Terry O'Hara
T: 809-777-9289
Heatwave is made with mango or papaya.

☐ **Hecho En Casa Pique Criollo**

GHSB p. 11
Hecho En Casa
Apartado postal 12223, Loiza
    Station
San Juan, PR 00914
T: 809-721-0982

☐ **Hell and Beyond Hot Sauce**

R4-17
Hell's Kitchen Food Products
1001 Page Street #2
San Francisco, CA 94117
William Eichinger
T: 415-255-7170

☐ **Hell in a Bottle Hot Sauce**

GHSB p. 103
Hell's Kitchen Food Products
See above

☐ **Hellfire & Damnation**

B5-2, GHSB p. 103
El Paso Chile Company
See Desert Pepper, p. 13

☐ **Hiccuppin' Hot Sauce**

Y3-18
Ford's Foods, Inc.
See Bone Suckin' Sauce, p. 5

☐ **Holy City Heat**

Y4-7, GHSB p. 103
Atlantis Coastal Foods, Inc.
See Bubba Brand H'eatin Hot
    Sauce, p. 6

☐ **Holy Habañero!**

R7-14, GHSB p. 104
Brown Adobe, Inc.
200 Lincoln Avenue, Suite 130
Phoenixville, PA 19460
Julienne Brown
T: 610-935-8588   F: 610-935-3484
E: jb419Aphilly.infi.net
W: BrownAdobe.com

☐ **Hoot Mon Hot Mustard**

GHSB p. 87
Hot Head Sauceworks
625 Elk Lane
Deep Gap, NC 28618
Ted Clevenger
T: 800-492-4687
E: hothead@appstate.campus.mci.net

☐ **Hot As Hell**

B3-9, GHSB p. 104
Cosmopolitan Foods
See Cosmopolitan Sambal, p. 11

☐ **Hot Bitch at the Beach**

R7-6, GHSB p. 108
Peppers
See Another Bloody Day in
   Paradise, p. 2

☐ **Hot Buns at the Beach**

R3-5, GHSB p. 108
Peppers
See Another Bloody Day in
   Paradise, p. 2

☐ **Hot Kechita**

R5-1, GHSB p .109
Hot Heads, Inc.
See Achiote Indian Sauce, p. 1

☐ **Hot Lava**

B2-11, GHSB p. 40
Little Freddy's
22151 US 19 North
Clearwater, FL 34625
Fred Lewis
T: 813-791-1118   F: 813-791-4092

☐ **Hot Licks**

Y5-13, GHSB p. 11
Dave's Gourmet
See Dave's Hurtin' Habanero
   Sauce, p. 12
The original label is in GHSB.

☐ **Hot Mama's Jalapeño Sauce**

GHSB p. 109
Hot Mama's
Box 44433
Phoenix, AZ 85064-4433
Donald L. Egger
T: 800-626-2707   F: 602-285-0115

☐ **Hot Sauce Harry's Dynamite
Hot Sauce**

GHSB p. 56
Hot Sauce Harry's
See Bob Harris Hot Ideas Hot
   Sauce, p. 5

☐ **Hot Sauce Harry's Habañero
Hot Sauce**

GHSB p. 56
Hot Sauce Harry's
See Bob Harris Hot Ideas Hot
   Sauce, p. 5

☐ **Hot Southern Nights**

Y5-11
Williamsburg Foods
Williamsburg, VA 23187
T: 804-566-0930

Hot Stuff Jab Jab
B7-3, GHSB p. 104
Hot Stuff
P.O. Box 2210
Stuyvesant Station, NY 10009
David Jenkins
T: 800-WANT-HOT
E: hotstuffny@aol.com
*David pioneered NYC's first hot
shop, now closed.*

**Hot Wings Buffalo-style
Sauce**
R3-16
Hot Wings
5095 Lakeshore Road
Buffalo, NY 14075
T: 888-BUF-WING   F: 716-627-2181

Hot as Hell
B3-9
Cosmopolitan Foods
See Cosmopolitan, p. 11

Huy Fong Sambal Oelek
GHSB p. 70
Huy Fong Foods, Inc.
5001 Earle Avenue
Rosemead, CA 91770
Donna Lam
T: 818-286-8328   F: 818-286-8522

Huy Fong Tuong Ot Sriracha
B1-14, GHSB p. 71
Huy Fong Foods, Inc.
See above

**Huy Fong Tuong Ot Toi
Viet-nam**
GHSB p. 71
Huy Fong Foods, Inc.
See above

I Am On Fire! Ready To Die!
B3-9
Cosmopolitan Foods
See Cosmopolitan, p. 11

Ieeowch!!!
B4 7, GHSB p. 112
Good Eats Company
See Harissa, p. 20

Iguana Red Pepper Sauce
R2-13, GHSB p. 87
Half Moon Bay Trading Co.
476 Riverside Avenue
Jacksonville, FL 32202-4912
Tom Nuijens
T: 904-356-7338   F: 904-359-0808

Inner Beauty Hot Sauce
B6-10, GHSB p. 11
Last Resort
1271 Cambridge Street
Cambridge, MA 02139
Lisa White
T: 617-868-9139   F: 617-868-4278

Inner Beauty Real Hot Sauce
B4-19, GHSB p. 12
Last Resort
See above

☐ **Isla Vieques Caribbean 3-Pepper Hot Sauce**
GHSB p. 12
Spice from Paradise
P.O. 1496
Vieques, PR 00765
Jim and Diana Starke
T: 800-741-0848   F: 787-741-2700
The company recently changed its name from IVCC to Spice from Paradise.

☐ **Isla Vieques Caribe Fire**
B7-19, GHSB p. 12
Spice from Paradise
See above

☐ **Isla Vieques Hot N' Honey Sauce**
GHSB p. 12
Spice from Paradise
See above

☐ **Isla Vieques Mountain Herb Hot Sauce**
GHSB p. 13
Spice from Paradise
See above

☐ **Isla Vieques Pique**
GHSB p. 13
Spice from Paradise
See above

☐ **Isla Vieques Salsa Picante**
GHSB p. 12
Spice from Paradise
See above

☐ **Isla Vieques Sweet & Spicy Pepper Sauce**
GHSB p. 12
Spice from Paradise
See above

☐ **Isla Vieques Sweet Revenge**
R2-8
Spice from Paradise
See above

☐ **Island Heat**
B4-16, GHSB p. 13
Helen's Tropical - Exotics
3316B Hamilton Blvd, Suite B
Atlanta, GA 30354
Becky Corley
T: 404-762-7767   F: 404-762-7767

☐ **Island Style Jamaican**
R5-7, GHSB p. 14
Island Style Foods, Inc.
50 Live Oak Drive
Holbrook, NY 11741
Douglas Canton
T: 516-472-3353   F: 516-472-3014

☐ **Island Treasure Jamaica Wildfire**
GHSB p. 14
Anjo's Imports
Box 4031
Cerritos, CA 90703
Lloyd Webster
T: 310-865-9544   F: 310-865-9544

☐ **Island Treasure Papaya Pepper Sauce**
B4-6
Anjo's Imports
See above

☐ **Jamaica Best Scotch Bonnet Pepper Sauce**

R3-15
Sunburst Commodity Trading
Sheephurst Lane, Marden
Tonbridge, Kent, U.K. TN12 9NS

☐ **Jamaica Hell Fire Doc's Special**

B6-3, GHSB p. 14
Jamaica Hell Fire
4625 North Manhattan
   Avenue, Suite J
Tampa, FL 33614
Frederick Johnston
T: 813-870-0899   F: 813-870-3473

☐ **Jamaica Hell Fire Hot Pepper Concentrate**

B5-10
Jamaica Hell Fire
See above

☐ **Jamaican Gourmet Hot Sauce**

Y3-4
Jamaican Gourmet
P.O. Box 43
East Aurora, NY 14052
Audrey McLean
T: 716-652-5803

☐ **Jo B's Chile Granatus Hot Chile Sambal**

GHSB p. 71
Jo B's, Inc.
Box 316
Warren, VT 05674-0316
Joanna Jenkins
T: 800-496-7889

☐ **Jo B's Chilipaya Island Rojo Sauce**

Y2-19, GHSB p. 15
Jo B's, Inc.
See above

☐ **Jo B's Gorda'sala Habañero Sauce**

GHSB p. 15
Jo B's, Inc.
See above

☐ **Johnny Wishbone Secret Sauce**

Y1-6
Johnny Wishbone Secret
   Sauce, Inc.
2472 Broadway, P.O. Box 388
New York, NY 10025
Peter Tuchman
T: 800-3-WISHBONE

☐ **Juanita's Picante Hot Sauce**

R4-16, GHSB p. 57
Juanita's Foods
645 North Eubank, P.O. Box 847
Wilmington, CA 90748
Bill Sneen
T: 310-834-5339   F: 310-835-1059

☐ **Jufran Pam-Pa-Gana Banana Sauce** ☆

GHSB p. 71
Jufran Inc.
Markina Metro
Manila, Phillipines

☐ **Jump Up & Kiss Me Hot Sauce with Passion**
B3-2, GHSB p. 15
Dave's Gourmet
See Dave's Hurtin' Habanero
Sauce, p. 12
The original label is on the poster.

☐ **Jump Up and Kiss Me Chipotle Sauce**
Y7-2, GHSB p. 15
Dave's Gourmet
See Dave's Hurtin' Habanero
Sauce, p. 12

☐ **Jump Up and Kiss Me Passionfruit Sauce**
Y4-5, GHSB p. 15
Dave's Gourmet
See Dave's Hurtin' Habanero
Sauce, p. 12

☐ **Justin Wilson's Jalapeño Sauce**
Y3-12
Cansa Foods, Inc.
P.O. Drawer 34D, 1822 15th Street
Gulfport, MS 39502
Jarrell Evans
T: 800-699-1307   F: 601-868-5551

☐ **KSOP Hot Country**
YR-3
Hot Sauce Harry's
See Bob Harris Hot Ideas Hot
Sauce, p. 5
KSOP Hot Country commemorates America's first FM country station.

☐ **Kayak Jack's Survival Sauce**
Y1-12, GHSB p. 87
Islandman, Inc.
7 Mountain Street, P.O. Box 823
Vinalhaven, ME 04863
John Gasbarre
T: 800-711-9002   F: 207-863-2794
E: islandman@islandman.com
W: islandman.com

☐ **Key West's Island Pepper Sauce**
Y7-1, GHSB p. 16
Key West's SOB, Inc.
1838 Patterson Avenue, Bldg P Unit 1
Deland, FL 32724
Candy Berg-Borror
T: 352-732-9148

☐ **Key West Really Really Hot Sauce**
R3-3
Jones Productions
Box 362
Key West, FL 33041
Trish Jones
T: 305-296-1863

☐ **Key West's S.O.B. Jamaican Hot Sauce**
GHSB p. 16
Key West's SOB, Inc.
See Key West's Island Pepper
Sauce, p. 26

☐ **Kitten's Big Banana Habañero Hot Sauce**
Y3-16
PepperTown
See Bad Girls in Heat, p. 3

Krista's Jamaican Hot Sauce
Y6-1
Krista's Kitchen
647 Ridge Road
Lackawanna, NY 14218
T: 716-825-0619

La Anita Hot Pepper Sauce
B3-6
La Anita Hot Pepper Sauce
Condimentos La Anita
Merida, Yucatan, Mexico

La Botanera
R2-12, GHSB p. 57
Mega Alimentos S.A. De C.V.
Antiguo Camino A Villa De Garcia
111
Apart. Post. 191 CP66350, Santa
Catarina, N.L., Mexico
Jesus Hernandez Barrera
T: 8-388-4300 F: 8-388-1200

La Guaca-Maya Botanera
R1-6, GHSB p. 57
Industries La Guaca-Maya
S.A.de C.V. Carretera A Navolato
#9105
Culiacan, Sin, Mexico
T: 60-00-61 F: 60-00-62

La Penca Salsa Picante
R6-8
La Penca
*I was unable to locate this
company.*

La Sabroza Chile de Arbol
GHSB p. 58
Monterrey Food Products
See Bufalo Jalapeño Mexican
Hot Sauce, p. 6

La Sabroza Chipotle
GHSB p. 58
Monterrey Food Products
See Bufalo Jalapeño Mexican
Hot Sauce, p. 6

La Victoria Taco Sauce
R2-14
Monterrey Food Products
3939 Cesar Chavez Avenue
Los Angeles, CA 90063-1899
Peter X. Galindo, Jr.
T: 213-263-2143 F: 213-263-2545

Last Rites
B7-10, GHSB p. 97
Hot Heads, Inc.
See Achiote Indian Sauce, p. 1

Lee Kum Kee Chili Oil
GHSB p. 72
Lee Kum Kee
304 South Date Avenue
Alhambra, CA 91803
Ernest Wong
T: 818-282-0337 F: 818-282-3425

Lee Kum Kee Fine Chili Sauce
R4-9
Lee Kum Kee
See above

27

☐ **Lee Kum Kee Singapore Chili Sauce**
GHSB p. 72
Lee Kum Kee
See above

☐ **Lingham's Chilly Sauce**
B1-1
Lingham & Son
SDN BHD
4870 Mak Mandin Industrial Estates
MK14 Butterworth P.W., Malaysia

☐ **Liquid Sky**
R2-3, GHSB p. 88
Wicked Good Sauce Co.
2046 Massachusetts Avenue
Cambridge, MA 01240
Jim Fahey
T: 617-864-2426

☐ **Lizano Chile**
GHSB p. 58
Productos Agroindustriales
del Caribe
S.A., San Antonio de Belin,
Heredia, Costa Rica

☐ **Lizano Chilero**
GHSB p. 58
Productos Agroindustriales
del Caribe
See above

☐ **Lizano Tabasco**
GHSB p. 58
Productos Agroindustriales
del Caribe
See above

☐ **Lol-Tun Habañero Peppers Hot Sauce**
Y2-6, GHSB p. 58
Lol-Tun
R. Flores Magon 486-D, Mexico,
DF06400

☐ **Lotta Hotta Besos de Fuego Fiery Pepper Sauce** ☆
Calido Chile Traders
See Calido Chile Traders, p. 7
This sauce has been discontinued.

☐ **Lotta Hotta Serrano Hot Pepper Vinegar**
Calido Chile Traders
This sauce has been discontinued.

☐ **Lottie's Bajan-Cajun Premium Hot Pepper Sauce**
GHSB p. 16
Pearl Imports
43 South Havenridge Drive
The Woodlands, TX 77381
T: 713-363-2358   F: 713-367-4825

☐ **Lottie's True Bajan Hot Pepper Sauce**
GHSB p. 17
Pearl Imports
See above

☐ **Louisiana Crude Reserve Black Hot Sauce**
Y3-2
Fig Tree Food Distributors
See Asbirin Hot Sauce, p. 3

☐ **Louisiana Gold**
B1-5, GHSB p. 40
Bruce Foods Corporation
See Casa Fiesta, p. 9

☐ **Louisiana The Perfect
Hot Sauce**
B6-16
Bruce Foods Corporation
See Casa Fiesta, p. 9

☐ **Macarico Piri-Piri**
B6-15, GHSB p. 72
Do Mingos Ribeiro Macarico
Praia de Mira, Portugal

☐ **Mad Dog Inferno Hot Sauce**
Y4-11, GHSB p. 116
Ashley Food Company
14 Ames Street, Suite 306
Dedham, MA 02026
David B. Ashley
T: 617-251-9775   F: 617-461-9186

☐ **Mad Dog Liquid Fire
Hot Sauce**
B7-17
Ashley Food Company
See above

☐ **Mancha's Original Agent
Orange Sauce**
GHSB p. 98
Mancha's Restaurant
1207 South 20th Street
Birmingham, AL 35205
Rebecca Mancha
T: 205-939-3304

☐ **Mancha's Original Nuclear
Sauce**
GHSB p. 98
Mancha's Restaurant
See above

☐ **Mancha's Original Wimp
Sauce**
GHSB p. 88
Mancha's Restaurant
See above

☐ **Mango Creek Hot Pepper
Sauce**
Y2-8
Mango Creek Farms
P.O. Box 21557
Charleston, SC 29413-1557

☐ **Mar Isquera** ☆
GHSB p. 59
Mar Isquera
Productos Humaya Rio Ameca
   #1527
Co. Ejidal Culiacan
Sinaloa, Mexico

☐ **Margaret's Pepper Sauce**
R3-10
Margaret's Pepper Sauce
Box 124
St. Vincent, West Indies

☐ **Marie Sharp's Habañero
Pepper Sauce**
R7-16, GHSB p. 17
Stann Creek Valley Road
Belize
Marie Sharp
T: 305-477-2616   F: 305-477-1892

29

☐ **Marinda's West Indian Hot Sauce**
Y3-5, GHSB p. 17
Marinda's Agro Processing Co. Ltd
P.O. Box 1448
St Vincent, West Indies
Glenford Ralph
T: 809-456-1020   F: 809-457-2880

☐ **Matouk's Calypso Sauce**
GHSB p. 18
National Canners Ltd.
Box 399
Port-of-Spain, Trinidad, West Indies
Jeremy Matouk
T: 809-842-3091   F: 809-642-3063

☐ **Matouk's Hot Pepper Sauce**
GHSB p. 18
National Canners Ltd.
See above

☐ **Matouk's Hot Sauce**
GHSB p. 18
National Canners Ltd.
See above

☐ **Matouk's MP Flambeau Sauce**
GHSB p. 18
National Canners Ltd.
See above

☐ **Matouk's West Indian Hot Sauce**
B1-2
National Canners Ltd.
See above

☐ **Mayan Kut**
R6-5, GHSB p. 59
Hot Heads, Inc.
See Achiote Indian Sauce, p. 1

☐ **Mean Devil Woman Cajun Pepper Sauce**
Y7-14, GHSB p. 109
Cajun Radar Foods
37820 M-40 Highway
Paw Paw, MI 49079
Rob Johnston
T: 616-657-8112   F: 616-657-8142

☐ **Melinda's Amarillo Hot Mustard Pepper Sauce**
GHSB p. 18
Fig Tree Food Distributors
See Asbirin Hot Sauce, p. 3

☐ **Melinda's Extra Hot Sauce**
GHSB p. 18
Fig Tree Food Distributors
See Asbirin Hot Sauce, p. 3

☐ **Melinda's Hot Sauce**
B3-10, GHSB p. 18
Fig Tree Food Distributors
See Asbirin Hot Sauce, p. 3

☐ **Melinda's XXXtra Hot Sauce**
GHSB p. 18
Fig Tree Food Distributors
See Asbirin Hot Sauce, p. 3

☐ **Melinda's XXXtra Reserve**
GHSB p. 18
Fig Tree Food Distributors
See Asbirin Hot Sauce, p. 3

☐ **Mezzetta California Hot Sauce**

GHSB p. 60
G.L. Mezzetta, Inc.
1201 East MacArthur Street
Sonoma, CA 95476
Dale W. Lucas
T: 707-938-8388 F: 707-938-8304

☐ **Mezzetta California Twist & Shout Habanero Hot Sauce**

R5-14, GHSB p. 60
G. L. Mezzetta, Inc.
See above

☐ **Mida's Chilli Sauce**

GHSB p. 72
Mida & Co., Ltd.
P.O. Box 498
Calcutta, India

☐ **Mild Kechita**

R5-3, GHSB p. 109
Hot Heads, Inc.
See Achiote Indian Sauce, p. 1

☐ **Miss Anna's Hot Pepper Sauce**

Y2-2, GHSB p. 19
Miss Anna's
Kingshill
St. Croix, U.S. Virgin Islands 00851
Rosalie A. Denis
T: 718-434-8396

☐ **Miss V's Caribbean Hot Sauce**

GHSB p. 19
Miss V's Food Products
Box 2034
St. Croix, U.S. Virgin Islands 00851
Elizabeth Luciana
T: 809-778-9351 F: 809-778-9351

☐ **Mongo Hot Sauce**

GHSB p. 73
Garden Row Foods, Inc.
See Cafe Louisiane Hotter'n Hell
    Sauce, p. 7

☐ **Montezuma Aztec Hot Sauce**

B7-2, GHSB p. 60
Sauces & Salsas Ltd.
1892 Rear Oakland Park Avenue
Columbus, OH 43224-3628

☐ **Montezuma Devil's Tingle Hot Sauce**

B4-3, GHSB p. 105
Sauces & Salsas Ltd.
See above

☐ **Montezuma Habanero Hot Hot Hot Sauce**

R7-12, GHSB p. 61
Sauces & Salsas Ltd.
See above

☐ **Montezuma Toltec Fire Water**

R3-13
Sauces & Salsas Ltd.
See above

☐ **Montezuma Wild Pequin Hot Sauce**

B6-12, GHSB p. 61
Sauces & Salsas Ltd.
See above

☐ **Mosquito Coast Dead Men Tell No Tales**

R6-18, GHSB p. 88
Mosquito Coast
4644 Gandy Blvd. #7
Tampa, FL 33611
Glen Bonner
T: 813-837-8410   F: 813-837-8410

☐ **Mother's Mountain Fire Eater**

Y6-14, GHSB p. 89
Mother's Mountain
110 Wodville Rd.
Falmouth, ME 04105
Carol Tanner
T: 800-440-9891   F: 207-781-2121

☐ **Mother's Mountain Habañero Heaven Deadly Pepper Sauce**

GHSB p. 105
Mother's Mountain
See above

☐ **Mountainman Fire Roasted Habañero Sauce**

Y6-3
Catskill Mountain Specialties, Inc.
127 Church Hill Road
Eddyville, NY 12401
T: 800-311-FIRE

☐ **Mr. Spicy Tangy Bang**

GHSB p. 89
Lang Naturals
741 Namquid Drive
Warwick, RI 02888
David Lang
T: 401-848-7700

☐ **Mrs. Tull's Hot Sauce** ☆

R1-3, GHSB p. 19
P.O. Box 10940
St. Thomas, U.S. Virgin Islands 00801
Mrs. Tull
The label is different every time I spot it in the USVI.

☐ **Mrs. Dog's Dangerously Hot Pepper Sauce**

B3-5, GHSB p. 89
Mrs. Dog's Products
P.O. 6034
Grand Rapids, MI 49516
Julie Applegate
T: 616-454-2677   F: 616-774-0193
The original label is found on the poster.

☐ **Muirhead Dragon's Breath Habañero Sauce**

GHSB p. 90
Muirhead
Ringoes, NJ 08551
Edward Simpson
T: 800-782-7803   F: 908-782-7803

☐ **Muirhead Dragon's Breath Sherry Pepper Sauce**

GHSB p. 90
Muirhead
See above

☐ **Nali** ☆

Y4-2

Nali Foods Ltd.
P.O. Box 5767
Limbe, Malawi, C. Africa

☐ **Nel's Old Time Hot Curry Sauce**

R6-4

Tijule Co. Ltd.
30 Paisley Avenue, Palmers Cross
Clarendon, Jamaica, West Indies
Juliette M. Newell
T: 809-986-4873   F: 809-986-9680

☐ **Nel's Old Time Jerk Sauce**

GHSB p. 20

Tijule Co. Ltd.
See above

☐ **Nel's Old Time Scotch Bonnet Hot Sauce**

GHSB p. 20

Tijule Co. Ltd.
See above

☐ **911**

R7-14

Hot Heads, Inc.
See Achiote Indian Sauce, p. 1

☐ **911 Hot Sauce**

B4-9, GHSB p. 20

Sanctuary Much, Inc.
6280 West Oakton Street
Morton Grove, IL, 60053
Jan Van Blommesteyn
T: 847-470-9112   F: 847-470-8391

☐ **99%**

Y5-10

Calido Chile Traders
See Calido Chile Traders, p. 7

☐ **No Joke For Beginners Hot Sauce**

R5-2, GHSB p. 90

Zavala Enterprises
11303 East Montgomery Drive #1
Spokane, WA, 99206-6683
Jesse Zavala
T: 509-922-6671

☐ **No Joke Hot Sauce**

GHSB p. 90

Zavala Enterprises
See above

☐ **Noh Korean Hot Sauce**

GHSB p. 73

Noh Foods International
P.O. Box 8392
Honolulu, HI 96815

☐ **Nor'Easter**

Y2-13

McNeill Inc.
See Doc McNeill, p. 14

☐ **Oak Hill Farms Herb & Garlic Hot Sauce**

GHSB p. 90

Oak Hill Farms
3264 McCall Drive
Atlanta, GA 30340
Ross Glover
T: 800-878-7808   F: 770-457-4546

☐ **Oak Hill Farms Three Pepper Lemon Hot Sauce**
GHSB p. 90
Oak Hill Farms
See above

☐ **Oak Hill Farms Vidalia Onion Hot Sauce**
GHSB p. 90
Oak Hill Farms
See above

☐ **Oochie's Red Neck Hot Stuff**
B1-15
Mayco Foods
3900 Joe Ashton Road
St. Augustine, FL 32092
Aubrey N. May
T: 904-829-5564   F: 904-797-8606

☐ **Original Louisiana Hot Sauce**
GHSB p. 41
Bruce Foods Corporation
See Casa Fiesta, p. 9

☐ **Outerbridge's Original Devilishly Hot Sherry Peppers Sauce**
R3-11, GHSB p. 21
Outerbridge Peppers Ltd.
Box FL 85
Flatts, FL BX, Bermuda
Yeaton D. Outerbridge
T: 809-293-0259   F: 809-293-2810

☐ **Outerbridge's Original Sherry Peppers Sauce**
B7-12, GHSB p. 20
Outerbridge Peppers Ltd.
See above

☐ **Outerbridge's Original Sherry Rum Peppers Sauce**
GHSB p. 21
Outerbridge Peppers Ltd.
See above

☐ **Ozone Shooter Tomatillo Serrano Sauce**
Y6-15, GHSB p. 61
Jeffrey's Restaurant
See Endorphinator Mango BBQ Sauce, p. 15

☐ **Pa Chai Buffalo Wing Sauce**
Y3-9
Yadkin Point Farms
P.O. Box 313
257 Woltz Lane
Advance, NC 27006
Howell Woltz
T: 910-998-9518   F: 800-836-6692
E: hwoltz@ols.net

☐ **Pain is Good Batch #114 Jamaican Hot Sauce**
Y3-7
Calido Chile Traders
See Calido Chile Traders, p. 7

☐ **Pain is Good Batch #37 Hot Sauce**
Y6-17, GHSB p. 112
Calido Chile Traders
See Calido Chile Traders, p. 7

☐ **Panda Brand Lee Kum Kee Hot Chili Sauce**
GHSB p. 73
Lee Kum Kee
See Lee Kum Kee Chili Oil, p. 27

☐ **Panda Premium Lee Kum Kee Sambal Oelek**
R3-7, GHSB p. 74
Lee Kum Kee
See Lee Kum Kee Chili Oil, p. 27

☐ **Panda Sriracha Chili Sauce**
GHSB p. 74
Lee Kum Kee
See Lee Kum Kee Chili Oil, p. 27

☐ **Panola 10 Point Hot Sauce**
B7-16, GHSB p. 110
Panola Pepper Corporation
See Bat's Brew, p. 4

☐ **Panola Cajun Hot Sauce**
GHSB p. 41
Panola Pepper Corporation
See Bat's Brew, p. 4

☐ **Panola Cajun Jalapeno Sauce**
B6-17, GHSB p. 41
Panola Pepper Corporation
See Bat's Brew, p. 4

☐ **Panola Extra Hot Hot Sauce**
GHSB p. 42
Panola Pepper Corporation
See Bat's Brew, p. 4

☐ **Panola Extra Hot Sauce**
B5-13, GHSB p. 42
Panola Pepper Corporation
See Bat's Brew, p. 4

☐ **Panola Gourmet Pepper Sauce**
B3-7, GHSB p. 41
Panola Pepper Corporation
See Bat's Brew, p. 4

☐ **Panola Green Tabasco Peppers**
GHSB p. 42
Panola Pepper Corporation
See Bat's Brew, p. 4

☐ **Panola Jalapeño Pepper Sauce**
B2-17
Panola Pepper Corporation
See Bat's Brew, p. 4

☐ **Pantainorasingh Sweet Chilli Sauce** ☆
GHSB p. 74
Pantainorasingh Manufacturer
196/3-4 Pradhipat Road
Bangkok, 10400, Thailand, 279 1342

☐ **Papa Joc**
B4-1, GHSB p. 21
Alimentos Kamuk
9th Avenue #1335
Gustavo Chinchilla, Costa Rica
0115062338439
T: 011-506-223-427

☐ **Pasa Salsa Picante** ☆
GHSB p. 62
Panamericana Abarrotera S.A. de
C.V.
Lago Athabaska 164 C
Colhuichapan, 11290,
San Salvador
T: 3995390 F: 3991476

☐ **Pearl's Hot Pepper Sauce**
Y7-18, GHSB p. 21
Pearl's Kitchen Products
P.O. Box 1639
Georgetown, St. Vincent
West Indies

☐ **Pee Wee's Cajun Cayenne Juice**
BR-2
All Cajun Food Company
See Andre's Rouge, p. 2

☐ **Pee Wee's Green Spiced Pepper Sauce**
GHSB p. 43
All Cajun Food Company
See Andre's Rouge, p. 2
This sauce is the same as the one above, renamed.

☐ **Pepper Creek Farms Jalapeño TNT**
GHSB p. 91
Pepper Creek Farms
1002 SW Ard Street
Lawton, OK 73505
Craig Weissman
T: 405-536-1300   F: 405-536-4886

☐ **Pepper Creek Farms Wildfire**
B2-16
Pepper Creek Farms
See above

☐ **Pepper Plant Chipotle Sauce**
GHSB p. 91
The Pepper Plant
P.O. Box 1119
Atascadero, CA 93423
Bob Roush
T: 800-541-4355   F: 805-466-9314

☐ **Pepper Plant Hot Pepper Sauce**
GHSB p. 91
The Pepper Plant
See above

☐ **Pepper Plant Hot Pepper Sauce with Garlic**
GHSB p. 91
The Pepper Plant
See above

☐ **Petit Tabasco** ☆
Y3-6
Bon Appetit S.A. de C.V.
El Salvador

☐ **Pick-a-Pepper Pepper Sauce**
R4-2, GHSB p. 21
Splendid Foods Limited
Lot 21C, I.D.C
O'Meara Industrial Estate, Arima
Trinidad, West Indies
T: 809-642-3203

☐ **Pickapeppa Pepper Sauce**
R7-3, GHSB p. 22
Pickapeppa Company
Shooters Hill, Jamaica
West Indies
Michael Lyn Kee Chow
T: 809-962-2928   F: 809-962-1863

☐ **Pickapeppa Sauce**

B6-13
Pickapeppa Company
See above

☐ **Pico Pica Hot Sauce**

R4-12, GHSB p. 62
Pico Pica Foods
P.O. Box 481
Harbor City, CA 90710

☐ **Pili Hot Pepper Condiment**

B6-5, GHSB p. 74
GTL, Inc.
112 Rittenhouse Street NW
Washington, DC 20011
Beverly G. Lochard
T: 202-723-6225   F: 202-861-6936

☐ **Pirate's Blend Caribbean Condiment**

R4-6, GHSB p. 22
Half Moon Bay Trading Co.
See Iguana Red Pepper
   Sauce, p. 23

☐ **Popie's Hotter'n Hell Sauce** ☆

R5-8
Garden Row Foods
See Cafe Louisiane Hotter'n Hell
   Sauce, p. 7
*This is now called Cafe Louisiane
Hotter'n Hell Sauce.*

☐ **Popie's Original Gourmet Cajun Hot Sauce** ☆

R6-1
Garden Row Foods, Inc.
See Cafe Louisiane Hotter'n Hell
   Sauce, p. 7
This sauce has been discontinued.

☐ **Prairie Fire Hot Pepper Sauce**

Y6-20
Sure Fire Imports Ltd.
1529 12 Avenue SW
Calgary, Alberta, T3C OR1, Canada
Fred Swift
T: 800-215-8913   F: 403-229-2111
E: fswift@direct.ca

☐ **Pure Hell Hot Sauce**

R5-9, GHSB p. 105
Two Chefs
See Halfway to Pure Hell, p. 20

☐ **Pyramid Brand Red Pepper Sauce**

GHSB p. 75
Pyramid Brand
Turkey
I was unable to find the address.

☐ **Quest For Fire XXX Hot Sauce**

Y1-8
Calido Chile Traders
See Calido Chile Traders, p. 7

☐ **Raging Inferno Tamarind Habañero Sauce**

Y4-4

Tastes of the East, Ltd.
P.O. Box 194
Syracuse, NY, 13207
Chef Shaikh
T: 800-CURRY-4-U   F: 315-471-2704

☐ **Ralph's Sweet Hot Sauce**

Y3-14, GHSB p. 91

Ralph's Gourmet Sauces
111 East Spencer Street, Suite #1
Ithaca, NY, 14850
Ralph Moss
T: 800-RSVPHOT   F: 607-277-6018

☐ **Rass Mon**

Y5-18, GHSB p. 22

Hot Head Sauceworks
See Hoot Mon, p. 22

☐ **Rasta Fire! Hot, Hot, Hot Sauce**

Y1-9

Fig Tree Food Distributors
See Asbirin Hot Sauce, p. 3

☐ **Rebel Fire No. 1**

B1-6, GHSB p. 92

Rebel Fire
247 Roxton Road
Toronto, Ontario, Canada, M6G3R1
Arnie Achtman
T: 416-530-0075   F: 416-530-1966
E: 103676.3206compuserve.com

☐ **Rebel Fire No. 3**

B1-6, GHSB p. 32

Rebel Fire
See above

☐ **Red Dog Tavern Armageddon**

R4-5, GHSB p. 116

Red Dog Tavern
South Shore Road, Box 192
Inlet, NY 13360
Edmond Klamm
T: 315-357-6500

The label changes at Ted's whim; he also doesn't like to answer the phone.

☐ **Red Dog Tavern Nuclear Waste**

B3-4, GHSB p. 98

Red Dog Tavern
See above

☐ **Red Rooster Louisiana Hot Sauce**

GHSB p. 43

Bruce Foods Corporation
See Casa Fiesta, p. 9

☐ **Redneck Gormay Sweet Thang**

Y2-4

Ruskin Redneck Trading Company
P.O. Box 1382
Ruskin, FL 33570
Dani or Sue Hellou
T: 813-645-7710   F: 813-641-1979

☐ **Rehobeth Beach Boardwalk Hot Sauce**

GHSB p. 92

Peppers
See Another Bloody Day in
  Paradise, p. 2

☐ **Religious Experience**

B5-17, GHSB p. 106

R.E. Foods
820 Struthers
Grand Junction, CO 81501
Jeff McFadden
T: 303-241-0975   F: 303-242-1021

☐ **Rica Red Banana Jama Sauce**

GHSB p. 23

Quetzal Foods International
P.O. Box 13643
New Orleans, LA 13643
Cody Jordan
T: 800-9FLAVOR

☐ **Rica Red Hot Pepper Sauce**

R3-8, GHSB p. 24

Quetzal Foods International
See above

☐ **Ring of Fire Habenero Hot Sauce**

R1-7, GHSB p. 62

Mike & Diane's Gourmet Kitchen
6755 Mira Mesa Boulevard,
  Suite 123, #204
San Diego, CA 92121
Michael Greening
T: 619-549-4809

☐ **Ring of Fire X-tra Hot Reserve Habenero Hot Sauce**

GHSB p. 62

Mike & Diane's Gourmet Kitchen
See above

☐ **Rio Diablo Hot Sauce**

R3-2, GHSB p. 63

Rio Diablo Hot Sauce, Inc.
151 South 1st St, Suite 100
Austin, TX 78704
Joe Dulle
T: 512-478-7669   F: 512-474-6087
*Aka Rio Diablo Mesquite-Smoked
Hot Sauce.*

☐ **River Run Hot Sauce**

Y3-13, GHSB p. 92

River Run
Main Street
Plainfield, VT 05667
Jimmy Kennedy
T: 802-454-1246   F: 802-454-8649

☐ **Road to Hell Hot Sauce**

R6-19, GHSB p. 106

Two Chefs
See Halfway to Pure Hell, p. 20

☐ **Rosie Coyote's Cilantro Green Chile Hot Pepper Sauce**

Y4-12

Rosie Coyote Sauce Co.
1829 West Bel Aire Court
Tucson, AZ 85705
Robert Keasing
T: 520-887-3883   F: 520-888-7008

☐ **Rowena's Red Lightning Hot Sauce**

R1-15, GHSB p. 93
Rowena's
758 West 22nd Street
Norfolk, VA 23517
Rowena J. Fullinwider
T: 800-627-8699   F: 804-627-1505

☐ **S.O.B.**

R4-3, GHSB p. 64
Hot Heads, Inc.
See Achiote Indian Sauce, p. 1

☐ **SLO JERK**

Y7-20
SLO JERK Gourmet Foods
11241 Johnson Avenue, Suite 301
San Luis Obispo, CA, 93401
Carlos O'Reilly
T: 800-SLOJERK   F: 805-995-3913
E: slojerk@aol.com
W: etropolis.slojerk.com

☐ **Salsa Huichol Hot Sauce**

R6-13, GHSB p. 63
Salsa Huichol
S de RL de CV av Rey Nayar, 31D
Los Fresnos, Tepic, Nay, Mexico

☐ **Salsa Picante de la Viuda**

R6-9
Productos Sane de
    Chapala, Zaragoza No. 389
Chapala, Mexico

☐ **Salu's Hot Reggae Sauce**

R6-3
Ethnic Int'l Export Inc.
P.O. Box 4
Kingston 4, Jamaica, West Indies

☐ **Salu's Jerk Sauce**

R7-11, GHSB p. 24
Ethnic Int'l Export Inc.
See above

☐ **Salu's Scotch Bonnet Pepper Sauce**

GHSB p. 24
Ethnic Int'l Export Inc.
See above

☐ **San Francisco's Famous Hunan Hot Sauce**

R5-12
Hunan Restaurant
924 Sansome Street
San Francisco, CA 94111
T: 415-956-7727

☐ **San Jorge Pique Tasco**

GHSB p. 44
Levapan S.A
Calle 153, 101-26
Bogota, Colombia

☐ **Santa Cruz Green Salsa**

GHSB p. 63
Santa Cruz Chili & Spice Co.
Box 177
Tumacacori, AZ
T: 520-398-2591

☐ **Santa Fe Exotic Green Chile Sauce**

B6-14

Santa Fe Exotic
Route 9, Box 56C
Santa Fe, NM 87501

☐ **Santa Fe Ole 3 Pepper Hot Sauce**

R5-17, GHSB p. 64

Santa Fe Ole
Box 2433
Santa Fe, NM 87504
Missy Fussell
T: 800-570-0724   F: 505-473-0724

☐ **Santa Fe Select Hell Raisin' Habañero**

Y4-10

Santa Fe Select
410 Old Santa Fe Trail
Santa Fe, NM 87501
T: 800-243-0353

☐ **Santa Maria Hot Chili Habañero Sauce**

GHSB p. 24

Nordfalks
P.O. Box 63, Neongatan 5, S-431 21
Molndal, Sweden
Raimo Orava
T: 4631674200   F: 46317760466

☐ **Santa Sauce Habañero Ho! Ho! Ho! Sauce**

Y2-14

Hot Sauce Harry's
See Bob Harris Hot Ideas Hot
   Sauce, p. 5

☐ **Satan's Revenge Chili Sauce**

B4-17, GHSB p. 106

Cosmopolitan Foods
See Cosmopolitan, p. 11

☐ **Satay Thai Red Chili Sauce**

Y6-4

Texas Food Research, Inc.
3202 West Anderson Lane, #203
Austin, TX 78757
Foo Swasdee
T: 800-352-1352   F: 512-467-0347

☐ **Scorned Woman Hot Sauce**

B4-13, GHSB p. 93

Oak Hill Farms
See Oak Hill Farms, p. 33
Comes in a black bag (see B4-14).

☐ **Scott's Jerk Sauce**

GHSB p. 25

Scott's Preserves
P.O. Box 94
Spanish Town, Jamaica, West Indies

☐ **Screamin' Demon**

Y3-17

South Side Pepper Company
320 North Walnut Street
Mechanicsburg, PA 17055
T: 717-691-7132   F: 717-691-8684

☐ **Screaming Sphincter Hot Sauce**

GHSB p. 113

Screaming Sphincter
1709 Avenue Q
Lubbock, TX 79401
Darren Jenks
T: 800-687-2272

□ **Selin Hot Pepper Souce**

GHSB p. 75

Selin Gida Sanayi Thalat
Mustafa Bey Cad No. 25, Karaoglu
 Apt K5D9
Alsancak 35220 XM, Turkey
T: 2324636967   F: 2324213794

□ **Sho Nuff New Orleans
Hot Stuff**

B2-12, GHSB p. 44

Cunningham Enterprises
3816 Duphine Street, Box 70586
New Orleans, LA 70172
Russ Cunningham
T: 504-566-1034

□ **Shotgun Willie's 2-Barrel
Habañero Sauce**

B7-8, GHSB p. 64

Jardine's Texas Foods
See Blazin' Saddle, p. 5

□ **Smack My Ass and Call Me
Sally Habañero Hot Sauce**

Y5-15

Tijuana Flats Burrito Company
7608 University Boulevard
Winter Park, FL 32792
Brian Wheeler
T: 407-673-2456   F: 407-306-0348

□ **So Damned Insane**

R2-5

Hot Heads, Inc.
See Achiote Indian Sauce, p. 1

□ **Sontava! The Original
Habañero Pepper Hot Sauce**

B5-12, GHSB p. 25

Jardine's Texas Foods
See Blazin' Saddle, p. 5

□ **Southern Spice Hot Sauce**

GHSB p. 44

Panola Pepper Corporation
See Bat's Brew, p. 4

□ **Southern Spice Jalapeño
Hot Sauce**

GHSB p. 44

Panola Pepper Corporation
See Bat's Brew, p. 4

□ **Southwest Spirit Smokin'
Oranges!**

Y3-3

RGE, Inc.
P.O. Box 23388
Santa Fe, NM 87502
T: 800-838-0773   F: 410-268-4957
E: jim@swspirit.com
W: swspirit.com

□ **Special Pepper Sauce** ☆

R1-14

A. Jack
Bequia, West Indies
T: 809-458-4100
*I found this sauce at a roadside
stand in Bequia.*

☐ **Spicy Caribee Tangy Pineapple Sauce**

GHSB p. 25
Spicy Caribee
154 Cristo Street
San Juan, PR 00902
Nereida Williams
T: 809-725-4690

☐ **Spicy Chesapeake Seafood Hot Sauce**

Y6-12, GHSB p. 110
Peppers
See Another Bloody Day in
Paradise, p. 2

☐ **Spitfire Hot Pepper Sauce**

B5-5, GHSB p. 26
Antilleo Foods
6080 Chabot Road
Oakland, CA 94618
Leander M. Hamilton II
T: 510-450-0123

☐ **Spitfire Red Hot Pepper Sauce**

GHSB p. 26
Antilleo Foods
See above

☐ **Sriraja Factory Chili Sauce**

B1-7
Sriraja Factory
1 Jermonjopol Road
Sriracha, Cholburi, Thailand

☐ **Stonewall Chili Pepper Co. Salsa Habañero**

B7-14
Stonewall Chili Pepper Co.
Box 241, Hwy 290 E
Stonewall, TX 78671
Jeff Campbell
T: 800-232-2995   F: 210-644-2377

☐ **Sunny Caribbee Hot Sauce**

B7-1, GHSB p. 26
Sunny Caribbee Spice Company
See Caribbee Pepper Sauce, p. 9

☐ **Sunny Caribbee XXX Calypso Hot Sauce**

GHSB p. 26
Sunny Caribbee Spice Company
See Caribbee Pepper Sauce, p. 9

☐ **Susie's Original Hot Sauce**

R5-4, GHSB p. 27
Susie's Hot Sauce
Upper North Street
St John's, Antigua, West Indies
Rosemarie McMaster
T: 809-461-4052

☐ **Swamp Island Extra Hot Cajun Hot Sauce**

Y7-13
Cansa Foods, Inc.
P.O. Drawer 34D, 1822 15th Street
Gulfport, MS 39502
Jarrell Evans
T: 800-699-1307   F: 601-868-5551

☐ **Sylvia's Hot Sauce**

B1-10

Sylvia's Food Products
332 Lenox Avenue
New York, NY 10027
Egypt Brown
T: 212-410-2106   F: 212-427-6389

☐ **Tabasco Pepper Sauce—
1865 version** ☆

Y4-19, GHSB p. 45

McIlhenny Company
Avery Island, LA 70513
Paul McIlhenny
T: 318-365-8173   F: 318-369-6326
E: tabasco.com

☐ **Tabasco Jalapeño Sauce**

R2-7, GHSB p. 45

McIlhenny Company
See above

☐ **Tabasco Spice Exchange
Pepper Sauce**

Y7-8

Fig Tree Food Distributors
See Asbirin Hot Sauce, p. 3

☐ **Tadpole's Hopping Hot Sauce**

Y4-17

New Mexico Classic Foods
P.O. Box 92485
Albuquerque, NM 87199-2485
T: 505-897-9556

☐ **Tahiti Joe's Polynesian
Hot Sauce**

Y5-12

Tahiti Joe's Hot Sauces
4310 State Drive
West Palm Beach, FL 33406
Joe Turner
T: 561-439-7832   F: 561-965-4909

☐ **Tamarindo Bay Pepper Sauce**

R7-19, GHSB p. 27

Half Moon Bay Trading Co.
See Iguana Red Pepper Sauce,
   p. 23

☐ **Tamazula Salsa Picante**

R6-12, GHSB p. 64

Salsa Tamazula
S.A. de C.V., Calle 22
   No. 2583, Zona Industrial
Guadalajara, Mexico

☐ **Tapatio Salsa Picante**

R4-15, GHSB p. 65

Empacadora Tapatio
2500 Fruitland Ave
Vernon, CA 90058
Luis Saavedra
T: 213-587-8933   F: 213-587-5266

☐ **Tasco Pepper Sauce** ☆

GHSB p. 45

Alimentos Regia S.A.
24 Avenue 30-39, Zone 12
Guatemala, 760616-17

☐ **Ted's Original Red Dog
Tavern Recipe #32**

Y2-10

Red Dog Tavern
See Red Dog Tavern, p. 38

☐ **Tennessee Boar's Breath Jalapeño Pepper Sauce**
Y7-16
Porky's Gourmet Foods, Inc.
315 10th Avenue North, Suite 106
Nashville, TN 37203
Ron Boyle
T: 615-244-PORK   F: 615-244-7427

☐ **Tennessee Red Lightnin'**
Y1-3
Porky's Gourmet Foods, Inc.
See above

☐ **Texapeppa Jalapeño Sauce**
GHSB p. 65
Jardine's Texas Foods
See Blazin' Saddle, p. 5

☐ **Texas Champagne Pepper Sauce**
BR1-13, GHSB p. 65
Jardine's Texas Foods
See Blazin' Saddle, p. 5

☐ **Texas Firecracker**
Y1-7, GHSB p. 56
Hot Sauce Harry's
See Bob Harris Hot Ideas Hot
  Sauce, p. 5

☐ **Texas Sweat Jalapeño Juice**
GHSB p. 65
Brazos Country Foods
See Brazos Beef Emporium, p. 6

☐ **Texas Tears**
B4-14, GHSB p. 113
Sgt. Pepper's Hot Sauce Micro
  Brewery
See Anne and Steve's Love Potion
  #1, p. 2
The original label is on the poster.

☐ **Texas Terminator Habañero Sauce**
GHSB p. 66
Jeffrey's Restaurant
See Endorphinator Mango BBQ
  Sauce, p. 15

☐ **The Brown Adobe Oso Hot!**
Y6-6, GHSB p. 51
Brown Adobe, Inc.
See Holy Habanero!, p. 21

☐ **The Brutal Bajan Hot Habañero Sauce**
Y2-1
Garden Row Foods, Inc.
See Cafe Louisiane Hotter'n Hell
  Sauce, p. 7

☐ **The Mean Green**
R5-13, GHSB p. 59
Hot Heads, Inc.
See Achiote Indian Sauce, p. 1

☐ **The Mex Hot Sauce**
B4-15, GHSB p. 60
The Mex
185 Main Street
Ellsworth, ME 04605
Sandra Wardwell
T: 207-843-6863

45

☐ **The S Bend Hot Pepper Sauce**

R2-6
E. Parris & Sons
N. R. Spencers, Barbados

☐ **The Wizard's Habañero Super Hot Stuff**

GHSB p. 94
Edward & Son's Trading Company
P.O. Box 1326
Carpinteria, CA 93013
Joel Dee
T: 805-684-8500   F: 805-684-8220

☐ **The Wizard's Hot Stuff**

R7-1, GHSB p. 94
Edward & Son's Trading Company,
See above

☐ **Three Banditos Salsa Habañero**

B1-12
Southwest Specialty Food Co.
See Ass Kickin' Hot Sauce, p. 3

☐ **Tia Juana Salsa Picante** ☆

GHSB p. 66
Ernesto Miramontes
Rio Tamesi 15A, Tijuana, Mexico

☐ **Tipica Jalapeno Sauce**

GHSB p. 27
Quetzal Foods International
See Rica Red Banana Jama
   Sauce, p. 39

☐ **Tipica Passion Fruit Hot Sauce**

GHSB p. 27
Quetzal Foods International
See Rica Red Banana Jama
   Sauce, p. 39

☐ **Tipica Pineapple Hot Sauce**

GHSB p. 27
Quetzal Foods International
See Rica Red Banana Jama
   Sauce, p. 39

☐ **Tipica Tamarind Hot Sauce**

GHSB p. 27
Quetzal Foods International
See Rica Red Banana Jama
   Sauce, p. 39

☐ **Tommy Tang's Seracha Chili Pepper Sauce**

GHSB p. 75
Aisha Spice, Inc.
708 North Gardner Street
Los Angeles, California 90046

☐ **Tongues of Fire**

Y4-1, GHSB p. 113
Garden Row Foods, Inc.
See Cafe Louisiane Hotter'n Hell
   Sauce, p. 7
The original label is in GHSB.

☐ **Trader Rick Bonny Pepper Island Hot Sauce**

GHSB p. 28
Trader Rick, Inc.
339 Saddlebrook Drive
Calhoun, GA 30701
Rick Engel
T: 706-625-8288   F: 706-625-8288

☐ **Trader Rick Mango/Tamarind Hot Sauce**

GHSB p. 28
Trader Rick, Inc.
See above

☐ **Trader Rick Mustard/Pepper Bajan Hot Sauce**

GHSB p. 28
Trader Rick, Inc.
See above

☐ **Trappey's Chef-Magic Jalapeño Sauce**

R5-6
McIlhenny Company
See Tabasco Pepper Sauce, p. 44

☐ **Trappey's Mexi-Pep Hot Sauce**

R4-1, GHSB p. 66
McIlhenny Company
See Tabasco Pepper Sauce, p. 44

☐ **Trappey's Mexi-Pep Louisiana Hot Sauce**

R7-8
McIlhenny Company
See Tabasco Pepper Sauce, p. 44

☐ **Trappey's Red Devil Cayenne Pepper Sauce**

R7-15, GHSB p. 46
McIlhenny Company
See Tabasco Pepper Sauce, p. 44

☐ **Trauma Super Hot Sauce,**

Y7-11, GHSB p. 99
Good Eats Company
See Harissa, p. 20

☐ **Trinidad Extra Hot Habañero Pepper Sauce**

B3-16, GHSB p. 28
Caribbean Food Products
1936 North Second Avenue
Jacksonvlle Beach, FL 32250
Carl F. Nelson
T: 904-246-0149   F: 904-246-7273
This sauce comes in several heat levels; the labels are essentially the same.

☐ **Trinidad Tropical Marinade & Grilling Sauce**

GHSB p. 28
Caribbean Food Products
See above

☐ **Triple Barn Burner**

R2-17, GHSB p. 29
Tropical Adventures Foods
2110405 Jasper Avenue #447
Edmonton, Alberta, Canada, T5J 3S2
Franklin Marshall
T: 403-424-5558   F: 403-421-4014

☐ **Tropical Chile Co. Caribbean Curry Hot Sauce**

Y7-4

Spice from Paradise
See Isla Vieques Caribbean
   3-Pepper Hot Sauce, p. 24

☐ **Tropical Tastes Extra Hot Sauce**

Y4-15, GHSB p. 29

Tropical Tastes
P.O. Box 1057
Summerfield, FL 34492
Liz Pingel
T: 904-245-3101   F: 904-245-3378

☐ **Try Me Cajun Sunshine Hot Pepper Sauce**

B7-18, GHSB p. 46

Wm. B. Reily & Company, Inc.
640 Magazine Street
New Orleans, LA 70130
Doug McDougall
T: 800-535-1961   F: 615-970-7681

☐ **Try Me Dragon Sauce**

GHSB p. 93

Wm. B. Reily & Company, Inc.
See above

☐ **Try Me Tennessee Sunshine Hot Pepper Sauce**

GHSB p. 46

Wm. B. Reily & Company, Inc.
See above

☐ **Try Me Tiger Sauce**

B7-15, GHSB p. 93

Wm. B. Reily & Company, Inc.
See above

☐ **Try Me Yucatan Sunshine Habañero Pepper Sauce**

R6-14, GHSB p. 66

Wm. B. Reily & Company, Inc.
See above

☐ **Turban Salsa Picante**

GHSB p. 29

Turban Brand Products, Ltd.
186 Eastern Main Road
Tunapuna, Trinidad, West Indies

☐ **Ultimate Burn**

Y4-13, GHSB p. 110

Peppers
See Another Bloody Day in
   Paradise, p. 2
Note the scratch-off bikini top.

☐ **Uncle Billy's VooDoo Jerk Slather**

B2-15, GHSB p. 30

Stache Foods
P.O. Box 174
Medomak, ME 04551
Stewart Blackburn
T: 800-255-8401

☐ **Uncle Fred's Habañero 150K Pepper Sauce**

Y7-3

Island Pepper Shack
320 North Alister
P.O. Box 659
Port Aransas, TX 78373
Fred Franklin

☐ **Uncle Willie's Heated Passion Jammin' Sauce**

GHSB p. 30

Uncle Willie's Inc.
P.O. Box 20008 West Village Station
New York, NY 10014
John Wilson
T: 800-789-6196

☐ **Uncle Willie's Hibiscus Vinegar**

GHSB p. 30

Uncle Willie's Inc.
See above

☐ **Uncle Willie's Jammin' Hot Sauce**

GHSB p. 30

Uncle Willie's Inc.
See above

☐ **Uncle Willie's Jammin' Mango Hot Sauce**

GHSB p. 31

Uncle Willie's Inc.
See above

☐ **Unlabeled bottle with wax top**

Y7-19

Tom's Coffee, Cards & Gifts
176½ Main Street
Binghamton, NY 13905
Thomas Kelleher
T: 607-773-8500

☐ **Uno**

B3-8, GHSB p. 31

Mayan Yours
101 Hope Road
Blairstown, NJ 07825
Kathleen Medore
T: 908-362-7825   F: 908-362-7925

☐ **Vampfire**

B6-11, GHSB p. 42

Panola Pepper Corporation
See Bat's Brew, p. 4

☐ **Vernon's Jamaican Jerk Sauce**

R7-17

Vernon's Jerk Paradise
252 West 29th Street
New York, NY 10001
Allan Vernon
May be out of business.

☐ **Vic's Original Fire Sauce**

R7-5, GHSB p. 94

Rodes Fresh & Fancy Market
3998 Bonita Beach Road
Bonita Springs, FL 33923
Ross Griffith
T: 800-786-0450   F: 813-992-2480

☐ **Virgin Fire Dragon's Breath**

GHSB p. 31
Virgin Fire
Box 37
St. John, U.S. Virgin Islands 00831
Bob Kennedy
T: 809-693-5937

☐ **Virgin Fire Eastern Caribbean Sauce**

GHSB p. 31
Virgin Fire
See above

☐ **Virgin Fire Hot Sweet Ting**

GHSB p. 31
Virgin Fire
See above

☐ **Virgin Fire Papaya Fire**

GHSB p. 31
Virgin Fire
See above

☐ **Virgin Fire Pineapple Sizzle**

B7-7, GHSB p. 31
Virgin Fire
See above

☐ **Virgin Islands Apocalyptic Hot Sauce**

R2-2, GHSB p. 99
Virgin Islands Herb & Pepper Co.
Box 9519
St. Thomas, U.S. Virgin Islands 00801
Richard Reiher
T: 809-776-2145

☐ **Vito's Hot Flash**

R4-8
Vito's Gourmet Market
206 South Elmwood Avenue
Buffalo, NY 14201
Vito Buscemi
T: 716-852-5650   F: 716-852-5850

☐ **Waha Wera (Burnt Mouth) Kiwifruit & Habanero Sauce**

Y2-9
Kaitaia Fire
SH.10, Lake Ohia
Kaitaia, New Zealand

☐ **Wajang Sambal Oelek** ☆

GHSB p. 76
Van Sillevoldt
Papendrecht, Holland

☐ **Walker's Wood Jerk Seasoning**

GHSB p. 32
Walker's Wood Marketing, Inc.
6187 Northwest 167th Street,
    Unit H29
Miami, FL 33015
Celia Dixon Chambers
T: 800-827-0769   F: 305-556-5879
E: walkers@caribplace.com

☐ **Walker's Wood Jonkanoo Pepper Sauce**

GHSB p. 32
Walker's Wood Marketing, Inc.
See above

☐ **Walker's Wood Scotch Bonnet Pepper Sauce**

Y2-12, GHSB p. 32
Walker's Wood Marketing, Inc.
See above

☐ **West Indian Trinidad Hot Sauce**

GHSB p. 33
Kwak Import Company
Bronx, NY 10474

☐ **West Indies Creole Classic Red Pepper Sauce**

GHSB p. 33
California-Antilles Trading
   Consortium
3446 Wilshire Terrace
San Diego, CA 92104
Richard E. Gardner
T: 619-295-6481

☐ **West Indies Creole Hot Pepper Sauce**

B4-4, GHSB p. 33
California-Antilles Trading
   Consortium
See above

☐ **Windmill Hot Pepper Sauce**

R4-4, GHSB p. 34
L.G. Miller & Sons Ltd.
Wildey, Barbados, West Indies
Patricia McLean
T: 809-427-4310   F: 809-429-2736

☐ **Windmill Red Hot Sauce**

B3-11, GHSB p. 34
L.G. Miller & Sons Ltd.
See above

☐ **Wing-Time Buffalo Wing Sauce**

Y1-10
Wing-Time
P.O. Box 919
Davis, CA 95617
Terence Brown
T: 916-753-0804   F: 916-753-5817

☐ **Wrong Number Chipotle Habañero Hot Sauce**

Y3-8
PepperTown
See Bad Girls in Heat, p. 3

☐ **Zack's Virgin Habañero Sauce**

GHSB p. 34
Zack's Foods
544 Nashville Pike, Suite 167
Gallatin, TN 37066
Mike Weeks
T: 615-822-9007   F: 615-264-3928

☐ **Ziyad Hot Red Pepper Sauce**

GHSB p. 76
Ziyad Brothers
5400 West 35th Street
Cicero, IL 60650
T: 708-222-8330

II.
Where To Find Sauces

While some of the most interesting sauces are still found at roadside stands and in bad neighborhoods of big cities, increasingly gourmet stores are featuring large sauce sections, and "hot" shops are proliferating. Call before you set out on an expedition to confirm whether those listed below are retail shops or strictly mail-order. (**Note:** stores are listed by state, and then alphabetically by city within each state.)

United States

Alabama

Caribbean Spice Company
8 South Church Street
Fairhope, AL 36532
T: 800-990-6088   F: 205-990-6088

Alaska

Salsa Vita
Sears Mall
600 East Northern Lights Boulevard
Anchorage, AK
T: 907-274-5830

Arizona

La Cocina Cookbook Company
750 East Sierra Madre
Gilbert, AZ 85296
T: 602-244-2207

Peppers & Spice
56 South Smoketree Blvd
Lake Havasu City, AZ 86403
T: 520-505-HOTT

Oak Creek Shirt, Nut & Cactus Co.
3128 West Thomas Road
Phoenix, AZ 85017
T: 602-956-7805

A J's Fine Foods
7141 East Lincoln Drive
Scottsdale, AZ 85253
T: 602-998-0052

Arizona Territory
7014 East Camelback Rd
Scottsdale, AZ 85251
T: 602-949-8805

Kokopelli
7091 East 5th Avenue
Scottsdale, AZ 85251
T: 602-994-1451

Señor Chile's at Rawhide
23020 North Scottsdale Road
Scottsdale, AZ 85255
T: 602-563-5600

Southwest Gourmet Gallery
320 North Highway 89A
Sedona, AZ 86336
T: 800-888-3483   F: 602-282-0686

Chile Pepper
201 Tubac Road
Tubac, AZ 85647
T: 800-441-8920

Garden Gate Gift Shop
Tucson Botanical Gardens
2150 North Alvernon Way
Tucson, AZ 85712
T: 602-326-9686

Gourmet Emporium
4744 East Sunrise
Tucson, AZ 85718
T: 520-299 5576

Territorial Gourmet
Calle Cerza
Tucson, AZ 85716
T: 520-297-9646

Totally Southwest
5575 East River Road
Tucson, AZ 85715
T: 520-577-2295

Santa Cruz Chile & Spice Co.
Old Tucson-Nogales Highway
Tumacori, AZ 85640
T: 520-398-2591

Arkansas

Great Southern Sauce Company
5705 Kavanaugh
Little Rock, AK 72207
T: 501-663-3338

California

Blazing Chile Brothers
3320 Trout Gulch
Aptos, CA 95003
T: 408-685-9040

Hot Lix
RR 6
Arroyo, CA 93421
T: 805-481-7015

Inyo Country Store
177 Academy Street
Bishop, CA 93514
T: 619-872-2552

Palisades Market
1506 Lincoln Avenue
Calistoga, CA 94515
T: 707-942-9549   F: 707- 942-6476

Jones & Bones Unlimited
621 Capitola Avenue
Capitola, CA 95010
T: 408-462-0521

Calido Chile Traders
North County Fair
200 East Via Rancho Parkway
Escondido, CA 92025
T: 619-489-5740

Chili Pepper Mania
1709-F Airline Highway
Hollister, CA 95023
T: 408-636-8259

El Lugar Caliente
510 Citrus Avenue
Imperial Beach, CA 91932

Hot Sauces
P.O. Box 1567
Jamestown, CA 95327
T: 209-984-4521

Sherwood's Lotsa Hotsa
P.O. Box 2106
Lakeside, CA 92040
T: 619-443-7982

Hot Licks
419 Shoreline Village Drive
Long Beach, CA
T: 310-437-8774

Hot Stuff
288 Argonne Avenue
Long Beach, CA 90803
T: 310-438-1118

Hot Hot Hot
473 Vista Gloriosa
Los Angeles, CA 90065
T: 800-959-7742
E: hothothot@earthlink.net

Salsa, Etc.
126 Great Mall Drive
Milpitas, CA 95035
T: 800-40S-ALSA

Monterey Seasons
711 Cannery Row
Monterey, CA 93940
T: 408-373-8415

Hot and Spicy Foods
P.O. Box 1986
Morgan Hill, CA
T: 800-64SPICY

Hot Sauce Hank
4000 Park Newport #300
Newport Beach, CA 92660
T: 714-759-8142

Ay Chihuahua
6702 San Pablo Avenue
Oakland, CA 94608
T: 510-566-9799

Hot Hot Hot
56 South Delacey Avenue
Pasadena, CA 91105
T: 800-959-7742
E: hothothot@Earthlink.net

Eagle Mountain Gifts
634 South China Lake Boulevard
Ridgecrest, CA 93555
T: 619-375-3071

Hot Pursuit
807 Via Presa
San Clemente, CA 92672
T: 714-492-5505

Bazaar Del Mundo
5433 Gaines Street
San Diego, CA 92110

Horton Plaza
1 Horton Plaza
San Diego, CA 92108
T: 619-235-4000

Hot Licks
865 West Harbor Drive
Seaport Village
San Diego, CA 92101
T: 619-235-4000   F: 619-669-1952

Some Like It Hot
3208 Scott Street
San Francisco, CA 94123
T: 415-441-7468

Salsas, Etc.
3683 Tunis Avenue
San Jose, CA 95132
T: 408-263-6392

Mo Hotta Mo Betta
P.O. Box 4136
San Luis Obispo, CA 93403
T: 800-462-3220   F: 805-545-8389

Ouchywawa! Hot Shop
2510B Main Street
Santa Monica, CA 90405
T: 800-WAWAWAS

2 Hot 4 It
539B Mission Drive
Solvang, CA 93463
T: 800-796-4657

Fire Alley
13207 Ventura Boulevard
Studio City, CA
T: 818-986-4328

Smith & Smith
71 Oak Street
Ventura, CA 93001
T: 800-567-7541

The Chile Cauldron
1641 Colusa Highway
Yuba City, CA 95993
T: 800-987-8512

Colorado

House of Fire
1108 Spruce Street
Boulder, CO 80302
T: 303-440-0929

Peppercorn
1235 Pearl Street
Boulder, CO 80302
T: 303-449-5847

The Hot Shop
114 South Main Street
Breckenridge, CO 80424
T: 303-453-2HOT

Colorado Spice Company
5030 Nome Street Unit A
Denver, CO 80239
T: 800-67SPICE   F: 303-373-9215

Garcia's
149 Steele Street
Denver, CO 80206
T: 303-388-7077

Old Santa Fe Pottery
2485 South Santa Fe Drive
Denver, CO 80223
T: 303-871-9434

The Chile Gourmet
3000 East 3rd Avenue
Denver, CO 80206
T: 303-331-9108

Calido Chile Traders
Southwest Plaza
8501 West Bowles Avenue
Littleton, CO 80123
T: 303-973-1433

El Mercado
137 Main Street
Longmont, CO 80501

Michele's Chile Pepper
P.O. Box 88021
Steamboat Springs, CO 80488
T: 303-870-1501

Calido Chile Traders
Westminster Mall
5513 West 88th
Westminster, CO 80030
T: 303-429-5051

Southwest Gifts & Salsa
P.O. Box 105
Windsor, CO 80550
T: 303-686-9982

Connecticut

Calido Chile Traders
Danbury Fair Mall
Danbury, CT 06810
T: 860-798-0855

Hay Day
1050 East Putnam Avenue
Riverside, CT 06878
T: 203-637-7600

Hay Day
1026 Post Road
Westport, CT 06881
T: 203-254-5200

Delaware

Peppers
2009 Highway 1
Dewey Beach, DE 19971
T: 800-998-FIRE

Florida

Calido Chile Traders
Brandon Town Center
2615 West Brandon Boulevard
Brandon, FL 33511
T: 941-403-0201

So You Like It Hot
220 NW 46th Street
Ft. Lauderdale, FL 33309
T: 904-878-0785

Pepperhead Quarters
314 First Street NW
Havana, FL 32333
T: 904-539-8020

American West Indies Trade — Key West
291 Front Street
Key West, FL 33040
T: 305-293-0305   F: 305-293-0154

Peppers of Key West
291 Front Street
Key West, FL
T: 305-295-9333

The Scoville House
5524 El Dorado Avenue
Lakeland, FL 33809
T: 813-858-0989

Calido Chile Traders
3404 Dean Street
Naples, FL 34104
T: 941-263-9403

Calido Chile Traders
1836 North Tamiami #10
Naples, FL 34102
T: 941-263-9403

Calido Chile Traders
Florida Mall
8001 South Orange Blossom Trail
Suite 776
Orlando, FL 32809
T: 407-339-7133

Calido Chile Traders
Seminole Town Center
247 Town Center Circle
Sanford, FL 32771
T: 407-321-4636

Fiery Food Junction
P.O. Box 189
Palmetto, FL 32220
T: 941-722-6772

Fire Station
P.O. Box 3162
Pinellas Park, FL 34664-3162
T: 813-547-1430

Dat'l Do-It Hot Shop
3255 Parker Drive
Saint Augustine, FL 32095
T: 800-468-3285

Jammin Ammon's Hot Shoppe
735 Dodecanese Bloulevard
Tarpon Springs, FL 34689
T: 813-944-2HOT

Georgia

Calido Chile Traders
Northpointe Mall
1000 Northpointe Circle
Alpharetta, GA 30202
T: 404-442-1778

Hot Stuff Inc
1147 Hardy Circle
Dallas, GA 30132
T: 404-521-0573

Redneck Gourmet
11 North Court Square
Newman, GA 30263
T: 404-251-0092

Chili Chompers
30 Barnard Street
Savannah, GA 31401
T: 912-234-1932

Chili Chompers
927A Main Street
Stone Mountain, GA 30086
T: 770-879-1709

Hawaii

It's Chihli in Hawaii
2080 South King Street
Honolulu, HI
T: 808-945-7070

Idaho

HOTT STUFF!
Boise Town Square
Boise, ID 83788
T: 209-322-7768

Illinois

International Hot Foods
905 North California Avenue
Chicago, IL 60622
T: 800-505-9999

Robert Adrian
2142 North Halsted
Chicago, IL 60614
T: 312-935-7335

Calido Chile Traders
107 West Jefferson Avenue
Naperville, IL 60540
T: 708-355-6814

Peoria HOT
1818 W. Teton Drive
Peoria, IL 61614
T: 309-691-8539

Calido Chile Traders
Old Orchard Shopping Center
374 Old Orchard Shopping
Skokie, IL 60077
T: 708-675-5348

Calido Chile Traders
Hawthorne Plaza
627 Hawthorne Center
Vernon Hills, IL 60061
T: 708-549-6442

Man That's Hot
810 West Governor Street
Springfield, IL 62704
T: 217-525-7584

Some Like It Hotter
404 West 53rd Street
Western Springs, IL 60558
T: 708-572-4503

Indiana

Calido Chile Traders
University Park Mall
6501 North Grape Road
Mishawana, IN 46545
T: 219-271-5531

Kansas

The Hot Spot
1 Riverfront Plaza #300
Lawrence, KS 66044
T: 913-841-7200

Calido Chile Traders
Oak Park Mall
11635B West 95th Street
Overland Park, KS 66214
T: 913-599-1228

Piquant Pepper
2605 East Douglas
Wichita, KS
T: 800-931-7474   F: 316-684-0990

Kentucky

Crow's Nest Hot Shoppe
7273 Dixie Highway
Louisville, KY 40258
T: 502-935-0752

Louisiana

Tabasco Country Store
McIlhenny Company
Avery Island, LA 70513
T: 800-634-9599

Bayou Country
600 Decatur Street #302
3rd floor
New Orleans, LA 70130
T: 800-406-3113

Creole Delicacies
1 Poydras Street
New Orleans, LA 70130
T: 504-523-6425

Tabasco Country Store
Riverwalk Marketplace
1 Poydras Street
New Orleans, LA 70130
T: 504-523-1711

The Hot Spot
5777 South Lakeshore Drive
Shreveport, LA 71119
T: 318-635-3581

Maryland

Kaufman's Fancy
The Market House
Annapolis, MD 21401
T: 410-269-0941

Sparky, Hoss and Duke's Hot Shop
4318 Rosedale Avenue
Bethesda, MD 20814
T: 301-657-FIRE

Burning Desires
10141 Sterling Terrace
Rockville, MD 20850
T: 301-990-1185

Flamingo Flats
406 Talbot Street
St. Michael's, MD 21663
T: 800-468-8841

Massachusetts

Le Saucier
Faneuil Marketplace
Boston, MA 02109
T: 617-227-9649

Cardullo's Gourmet Shoppe
6 Brattle Street
Cambridge, MA 02138
T: 617-491-8888   F: 617-876-5066

Nantucket Gourmet
4 India Street
Nantucket, MA 02554
T: 508-228-4353

Marty's Fine Wines & Gourmet
675 Washington Street
Newton, MA 02160
T: 617-332-1230

Guido's
1020 South Street
Pittsfield, MA 01201
T: 413-442-9912   F: 413-442-4984

Chile Head
23 Banks Street
Somerville, MA 02144
T: 800-4WE-BURN

Michigan

Clubhouse BBQ & Spice Co.
22020 Woodward Avenue
Ferndale, MI 48220
T: 810-548-8060

Some Like It Hot
14125 Riverside Drive
Livonia, MI 48154

Calido Chile Traders
Twelve Oaks Mall
27716 Novi Road
Novi, MI 48377
T: 810-305-7239

Hot Shoppe Hill
37820 M-40 Highway
Paw Paw, MI 49079
T: 616-657-8112   F: 616-657-8142

Calido Chile Traders
Lakeside Mall
14600 Lakeside Circle
Sterling Heights, MI48313
T: 810-695-6850

Calido Chile Traders
Grand Traverse Mall
3200 South Airport Road West
Traverse City, MI 49684
T: 810-695-6850

Minnesota

Calido Chile Traders
Mall of America
174 East Broadway
Bloomington, MN 55425
T: 941-403-0201

Calido Chile Traders
Mall of America
390 North Garden
Bloomington, MN 55425
T: 612-883-0240

Missouri

America's Favorites
1550 East Battlefield Road
Springfield, MO 65804
T: 800-454-2614

Calido Chile Traders
Union Station
1820 Market Street
St. Louis, MO 63103
T: 913-384-0019

Montana

Chips 'n Salsa
205 Showplace, Suite B
Belgrade, MT 59714
T: 406-585-5175

Fire on the Mountain
6300 Jackrabbit Lane
Belgrade, MT 59714
T: 406-388-1421

Peppers & Pasta
8 First Street East
Kalispell, MT
T: 406-257-4478

Uncle Bill's House of Hot Sauce
311 North Higgins Avenue
Missoula, MT 59802
T: 406-543-5627

Nevada

Calido Chile Traders
Boulevard Mall
3528 Maryland Parkway
Las Vegas, NV 89109

New Hampshire

Gourmet Sauce Works
145 Route 28 Bypass
Derry, NH 03038
T: 603-432-1684

New Jersey

Chile Today Hot Tamale
919 Highway 33
Freehold, NJ 07728
T: 800-468-7377

Chef's Choice
Princeton Market Fair
Princeton, NJ 08540
T: 609-452-7176

New Mexico

Chile Addict
1414 Eubank NE
Albuquerque, NM 87112
T: 800-CRY-CHILE

Chile Pepper Emporium
328 San Felipe NW
Albuquerque, NM 87104
T: 505-242-7538

Chile Patch USA
204 San Felipe NW (in Old Town)
Albuquerque, NM 87104
T: 800-458-0646

Fremont's
556 Coronado Center NE
Albuquerque, NM 87110
T: 505-883-6040

Potpourri
121 Romero NW
Albuquerque, NM 87104
T: 505-243-4087

Salsa Express
P.O. Box 3985
2432 Menaul NE
Albuquerque, NM 87190
T: 800-43SALSA F: 505-884-5266

Southwest Collection
5713 Madeira Place NE
Albuquerque, NM 87110
T: 505-884-3886

Chile Hill Emporium
Box 9100
Bernalillo, NM 87004
T: 505-867-3294

Hatch Chile Express
622 Franklin
Hatch, NM 87937
T: 505-267-3226

Calido Chile Traders
410 Old Santa Fe Trail
Santa Fe, NM 87501
T: 505-983-4800

Santa Fe Select
410 Old Santa Fe Trail
Santa Fe, NM 87501
T: 505-986-0454   F: 505-986-0640

The Chile Shop
109 East Water Street
Santa Fe, NM 87501
T: 505-983-6080   F: 505-984-0737

Coyote Cafe General Store
132 West Water Street
Santa Fe, NM 87501
T: 800-866-HOWL

New York

Vito's Gourmet Market
206 South Elmwood Avenue
Buffalo, NY 14201
T: 716-852-5650

Tabasco Chris
26 Cromwell Drive
Clifton Park, NY 12065
T: 518-383-2673

Barefoot Contessa
46 Newtown Lane
East Hampton, NY
T: 516-324-0240

The Hot Spot
451 White Plains Road
Eastchester, NY 10709
T: 914-961-4649

Lots of Hots & Fiery Foods
39 Pebble Hill Road
Fairport, NY 14450-2632
T: 800-836-1677

Pungent Pod
1 Ridge Street
Glens Falls, NY 12801
T: 518-743-0467   F: 518-793-3180

Premier Gourmet
3465 Delaware Avenue
Kenmore, NY 14217
T: 716-877-3574

The Saucy Chile Store
Hudson Valley Mall
Route 9W
Kingston, NY 12402
T: 914-336-0185

Dean & Deluca
560 Broadway
New York, NY 10012
T: 212-431-1619

Hot Stuff
P.O. Box 2210, Stuyvesant Station
New York, NY 10009
T: 800-WANTHOT
E: hotstuffny@aol.com

Kelley & Ping Asian Grocery
127 Greene Street
New York, NY

Kitchen
218 Eighth Avenue
New York, NY 10011
T: 212-243-4433

Pungent Pod
Aviation Mall
Queensburg, NY 12804
T: 518-793-3180

Hay Day
15 Palmer Ave
Scarsdale, NY 10583
T: 914-722-0200

The Hot Shoppe
142-144 Walton Street
One Armory Square
Syracuse, NY 13202
T: 315-424-1010

The Chile Factory
710 Horatio Street
Riverside Mall
Utica, NY 13502
T: 315-733-0977

North Carolina

A Southern Season
Eastgate Shopping Center
Chapel Hill, NC 27515
T: 800-253-3663   F: 919-942-9274

Calypso Queen
Box 35347
Charlotte, NC 28235
T: 704-527-1464

Hot Shots
3124 Pinehurst Place
Charlotte, NC 28209
T: 704-527-2422

Calido Chile Traders
Carolina Place
11025 Carolina Place Parkway
Pineville, NC 28134
T: 704-341-0777

Calido Chile Traders
Crabtree Valley Mall
4325 Glenwood Avenue
Raleigh, NC 27612
T: 919-510-8898

Ohio

Calido Chile Traders
Los Mercaderas
7813A. Main Street
Berlin, OH 44610
T: 330-893-3542

Pepper Head
Great Lakes Mall
Mentor, OH 44136
T: 216-846-3981

Hot Prospects
26747 Brookpark Road Extension
North Olmsted, OH 44070
T: 216-779-5099

Pepper Head
Marmatown Mall
7899 West Ridgewood Drive
Parma, OH 44129
T: 216-885-0302

Pepper Head
South Park Mall
Strongsville, OH 44136
T: 216-846-3981

Oklahoma

The International Pantry
1618 West Lindsey
Norman, OK 73069
T: 405-360-0765

The Pepper Place
614 West Main
Norman, OK 73069
T: 405-364-7617

Calido Chile Traders
1901 NW Expressway
Oklahoma City, OK 73118
T: 405-842-7676

Southwest Chili Traders
1901 NW Expressway
Oklahoma City, OK 73118
T: 406-842-7676

Calido Chile Traders
Woodlands Hills Mall
7021 South Memorial Drive
Tulsa, OK 74133
T: 918-252-2244

Pennsylvania

Hot or Not
Box 463 RR 6
Boyertown, PA 19512
T: 610-369-0130

Pepper Island Beach
1220 Valleyview Drive
Lawrence, PA 15055
T: 412-746-2401

Not Just Coffee
4229 Main Street
Manayunk, PA
T: 215-482-8582

South Side Pepper Co.
320 North Walnut Street
Mechanicsburg, PA 17055
T: 717-691-7132

Garden of Ogden Firey Foods
3115 Naamans Creek Road
Ogden, PA 19061
T: 215-284-3021

12th Street Cantina
Reading Terminal Market
45 North 12th Street
Philadelphia, PA 19107
T: 215-625-0321

Spice Terminal
Reading Terminal Market
12th & Arch Streets
Philadelphia, PA 19107
T: 215-592-8555

South Carolina

Calido Chile Traders
Haywood Mall
700 Haywood Road
Greenville, SC 29607
T: 864-627-1070

Chili Chompers
Coligny Plaza
Building 1, Space 8
Hilton Head, SC 29928
T: 803-785-5230

Tennessee

Fiery Foods
909 20th Avenue South
Nashville, TN 37212
T: 615-320-5475

Hot Stuff
900 8th Avenue North
Nashville, TN 37208
T: 800-738-9938

Texas

Central Market
4001 North Lamar
Austin, TX 78759
T: 512-206-1000   F: 512-206-1010

Sambet's Cajun Store
8644 Spicewood Springs Road, Suite F
Austin, TX 78759
T: 800-472-6238

Ralph's Fine Foods
6901 Snider Plaza
Dallas, TX 75205
T: 214-368-0931

Calido Chile Traders
West End Mall
603 Munger
Dallas, TX 75202
T: 214-969-7507

Hot Sauce Harry's
3422 Flair Drive
Dallas, TX 75229
T: 800-588-8979   F: 214-956-9885

Pendery's
1221 Manufacturing
Dallas, TX 75207
T: 800-533-1870   F: 214-761-1966

El Paso Chile Company
909 Texas Avenue
El Paso TX 79901
T: 800-274-7468   F: 915-544-7552

Chantilly's Gifts
21146 Highway 155 South
Flint, TX 75762
T: 903-825-2259

Calido Chile Traders
Hulen Mall
4800 South Hulen Street
Fort Worth, TX 76132
T: 817-370-2217

Calido Chile Traders
Houston Galleria III
5175 Westheimer
Houston, TX 77056
T: 713-753-4762

Island Pepper Shack
320 North Alister
Port Aransas, TX 78737
T: 888-862-5373

Calido Chile Traders
196 North Star Mall
San Antonio, TX 78216
T: 210-344-8670

Rivera's Chile Shop
109 ½ Concho Street in Market Square
San Antonio, TX 78207
T: 210-226-9106

Utah

The Heat Is On
602 East 500 South
Salt Lake City, UT 84102
T: 801-355-8264

Virginia

Sherwood Gourmet
7900 Andrus Road
Alexandria, VA 22306
T: 703-799-4041

Spices, Etc.
1712 Allied Street
Charlottesville, VA 22905
T: 804-293-9410

Added Touch
8393 Sudley Road
Manassas, VA 22110
T: 703-368-4118

Washington

Chiles Delux
P.O. Box 1425
Botnell, WA 98041-1425

Mango N Chili
9301A North Division
Spokane, WA 99218
T: 509-468-5292

Wyoming

The Whole Earth Grocery
111 Ivinson Avenue
Laramie, WY 82070
T: 307-745-4268

Canada

The Pepper Shack
R. E. I., Site 7, Box 54
Beaverlodge, Alberta T0H 0C0
T: 403-354-3125 F: 403-354-3124

Kaffe Coffee & Salsa House
2138 33rd Avenue SW
Calgary, Alberta T2T 1Z6
T: 403-240-9133

Nutter's Bulk & Natural Foods
900 Railway Avenue
Canmore, Alberta T0L 0M0
T: 403-678-3335 F: 403-678-4570

Louisiana Purchase
10320-111 Street
Edmonton, Alberta T5K 1L2
T: 403-420-6779

Pioneer Market
1405 Laurence Road
Kelowa, British, Columbia V1W4M6
T: 604-762-2544   F: 604-762-9278

Hot Pursuits
7384 4th Line Road RR #4
Kemptville, Ontario K0G 1J0
T: 613-489-2974

Chilly Chiles
P.O. Box 149
Navan, Ontario K4B 1J4
T: 800-448-5843   F: 613-835-3984

Pepperpot
105-123 Carrie Cats Court
Lonsdale Quay
North Vancouver,British Columbia
V7M 3K7
T: 604-986-1877

Red Mountain Market
P.O. Box 1258
Rossland, British Columbia V0G 1YO
T: 604-362-5556   F: 604-362-9531

The Chile Connection
3B Oneil Crescent
Saskatoon, Saskatchewan S7N 1W7
T: 306-477-0315   F: 306-221-9320

Elwood's Joint
3145 West Broadway
Vancouver, British Columbia V6K 2H2
T: 604-736-4301

Hot Lovers Fiery Foods
1282 Wolseley Avenue
Winnipeg, Manitoba R3G 1h4
T: 204-772-6418

Caribbean

Island Hoppers/Down Island Ventures
P.O. Box 37
Cruz Bay, St. John, USVI 00831
T: 809-693-7200

Sunny Caribbee Spice Company
Roadtown
Tortola, USVI 00803
T: 809-494-2178

England

TECMACO International
Unit C5, London Road
Thrupp Stroud, GL52BX
T: 441453731737   F: 441453731747

III.
Where To Eat Sauces

Below are restaurants that either celebrate hot sauces with great collections, or are run by people in the hot sauce business. For a complete listing of spicy restaurants across America that serve the kind of food that makes Mount St. Helens look cool, see my previous book, *Trail of Flame* (Ten Speed Press, 1995).

Alabama

Mancha's Restaurant
1207 South 20th Street
Birmingham, AL 35205
T: 205-939-3304
Rebecca Mancha makes Mancha's Original Agent Orange Sauce.

California

Firehouse Beach Cafe
722 Grand Avenue
Pacific Beach, CA 92109
T: 619-272-1999
Meals are served with a firebucket of sauces.

Chiletos Taqueria
440 East Ortega Street
Santa Barbara, CA 93101
T: 805-965-4545
Ten homemade salsas are made fresh daily.

Colorado

Firehouse Bar & Grill
1525 Blake Street
Denver, CO 80202
T: 303-820-3308
The chef here makes Firehouse Satan's Slow Burn.

Connecticut

Eli Cannon's Tap Room
695 Main Street
Middletown, CT 06457
T: 203-347-3547
There are as many hot sauces as beers to choose from.

Delaware

Starboard Restaurant
2009 Highway One
Dewey Beach, DE 19971
T: 302-227-4600
Chip Hansen has perhaps the world's largest sauce collection; bring a new sauce and get a free lunch.

District of Columbia

Red Sage
605 14th Street NW
Washington, DC
T: 202-638-4444
*Red Sage is owned by Mark
Miller, maker of Coyote Cocina sauces.*

Rockland's - Washington's BBQ
2418 Wisconsin Avenue
Washington, DC 20007
T: 202-333-2558
*John Snedden has a display called a
"Wall of Flame" which features his
great sauce collection.*

Florida

Barnacle Bill's
14 Castillo Drive
St Augustine, FL 32085
T: 904-824-3663
*Owner Chris May is the maker of Dat'l
Do It sauces.*

Illinois

Heaven on Seven
111 North Wabash (7th floor)
Chicago, IL 60602
T: 312-263-6443
*Chef Jimmy Bannos has a huge sauce
collection; bring in a new sauce and
get a free lunch.*

Iowa

Big Daddy's Bar-B-Q
1000 East 14th Street
Des Moines, IA 50316
T: 515-262-0352
Ask about Big Daddy's challenge.

Kentucky

Gib's Smoke House & Grill
2224 Dundee Road
Louisville, KY 40205
T: 502-451-5154
Maker of Gib's Nuclear Hell Sauce.

Louisiana

Cafe Louisiane
2246 South Acadian Thruway
Baton Rouge, LA 70808
T: 504-343-2148
*Cafe Louisiane is the former owner of
Cafe Louisiane sauce.*

K-Paul's Louisiana Kitchen
416 Chartres Street
New Orleans, LA 70130
T: 504-524-7394
This is Paul Prudhomme's restaurant.

Maine

The Mex
185 Main Street
Ellsworth, ME 04605
T: 207-667-4494
*Owners Sandy and Bruce Wurdwell
make The Mex hot sauce.*

Maryland

Cultured Pearl
1116 Hollins Street
Baltimore, MD 21223
T: 410-837-1947
Cultured Pearl sponsors an annual Hot Sauce and Salsa Tasting Festival.

Massachusetts

East Coast Grill
1271 Cambridge Street
Cambridge, MA 02139
T: 617-491-6568
The East Coast Grill is where Inner Beauty originated.

Porter House Cafe
2046 Massachusetts Avenue
Cambridge, MA 02138
T: 617-354-9793
This is the home of Jimmy Fahey's Liquid Sky hot sauce.

New Mexico

Coyote Cafe
132 West Water Street
Santa Fe, NM 87501
T: 505-983-1615
Owner Mark Miller makes Coyote Cocina sauces.

New York

Red Dog Tavern
South Shore Road
Inlet, NY 13360
T: 315-357-6500
Red Dog Tavern makes Armageddon sauce; ask Ted about his challenge.

Seventh Lake House
On the Seventh Lake
Inlet, NY 13360
T: 315-357-6028
Seventh Lake House sponsors a "Fire and Spice Night" every May.

Acme Bar & Grill
9 Great Jones Street
New York, NY 10012
T: 212-420-1934
Acme has a terrific hot sauce collection and bottles its own sauce.

Dinosaur Bar-B-Q
246 West Willow Street
Syracuse, NY 13202
T: 315-476-4937
Dinosaur's Devils Duel is made at this biker bar.

North Carolina

Flying Burrito
746 Airport Road
Chapel Hill, NC 27514
T: 919-967-7744
Owners Phil and Vicki Campbell make Flying Burrito Flounder Juice.

Flying Burrito
Durham Athletic Park
Durham, NC (seasonal)
*Owners Phil and Vicki Campbell make
Flying Burrito Flounder Juice.*

On the Verandah
Highway 64 West
Highlands, NC (seasonal)
T: 704-526-2338
They have a large hot sauce collection.

Chilli Peppers
3001 North Croatan Highway
Kill Devil Hill, NC 27948
T: 919-441-8081
They make Chilli Peppers hot sauce.

Texas

Jeffrey's Restaurant
1204 West Lynn Street
Austin, TX 78703
T: 512-477-5584
*Chef David Garrido makes Texas
Terminator and other fine hot sauces.*

Seis Salsas
2004 South 1st Street
Austin, TX 79602
T: 512-346-9990
Count 'em.

Vermont

Bourbon Street Grill
213 College Street
Burlington, VT 05401
T: 802-865-2800
*Chef Art O'Connor makes Bourbon
Street Fire Sauce.*

River Run Restaurant
3 Main Street
Plainfield, VT 05667
T: 802-454-1246
*Chef Jimmy Kennedy has a good sauce
collection; he also makes River Run
hot sauce.*

Sam Rupert's
69-6 RR 1
Warren, VT 05674
T: 802-583-2421
*Sam Rupert sponsors a "Some Like It
Hot" festival every fall.*

IV.
Festivals

Hot & Spicy Tasting Day
A Taste of Thailand
Restaurant
215 East Walnut Street
Des Moines, IA
T: 515-282-0044

Chilli Festival
The Fragrant Garden
Erina, NSW Australia
T: 043-677322

Hava-Salsa Challenge
Windsor State Park Beach
Lake Havasu, AZ
T: 602-453-3641

Hot & Spicy Weekend
Mohonk Mountain
House
Lake Mohonk
New Paltz, NY
T: 800-772-6646

Fire and Spice Night
Seventh Lake House
Seventh Lake
Inlet, NY 13360
T: 315-357-6028 (ask for Jim Holtz)

Miller Genuine Draft Hot & Spicy Food Festival
Marietta, GA
T: 404-872-4731 (ask for Bill Averill)

Austin Chronicle Hot Sauce Contest
Travis County Farmer's
Market
Austin, TX
T: 512-454-5766

San Jose Chile Pepper Festival
San Jose, CA
T: 408-298-3202

Chile & Frijole Festival
Pueblo CO
T: 800-233-3446

Hatch Chiles Festival
Hatch Fairgrounds
Hatch, NM
c/o Chamber of
Commerce
T: 505-267-5050
Alternate: 505-267-4847

Hot Licks Hot Sauce Festival
Seaport Village
San Diego, CA
T: 619-543-0243

Mencken's Cultured Pearl Cafe's Hot Sauce and Salsa Tasting Festival
Baltimore, MD
T: 410-332-9962

Northwest Fiery Foods Festival
Pasco, WA
T: 509-544-9436

Santa Fe Wine and Chile Fiesta
Santa Fe, NM
T: 505-983-7929

Chile Pepper Fiesta
Brooklyn Botanic
Garden
Brooklyn, NY
T: 718-622-4433

La Fiesta de los Chiles
Tucson Botanical
Gardens
Tucson AZ
T: 602-326-9686

Pepper Festival
St. Martinville, LA
T: 318-394-9704

Pig & Pepper Festival
Kimball's Farm
Westford, MA
T: 508-369-0366
E: gsoucy@usa1.com

November

Some Like It Hot
Sam Rupert's Restaurant
69-6 RR1
Warren, VT 05674
T: 802-583-2421

**CASI Terlingua
International Chili
Championship**
Terlingua, TX
T: 817-365-2504 or
806-352-8783

**Original Viva
Terlingua Fowler
Memorial Cookoff**
Terlingua, TX
T: 903-874-5601

Web Listings

There are hundreds of chile-related web sites that are easily accessed through various search engines. To get you started, however, I've listed a few — which offer links to a maze of other sites online. Web addresses are also listed under Hot Sauce Manufacturers (p. 1).

Chile-Heads Home Page
http://neptune.netimages.com/~chile

Cybersauce (a funny home page — about a virtual sauce)
http://www.cybersauce.com/

Fire Zone America's Favorites
http://www.truck.net/store/affire.html

Habanero Studios (recipes)
http://www.habaneros.com/

Heat Me Up (recipes, hot links, etc.)
http://www.heatmeup.com/

Hottest Pepper (Scoville scales for chiles)
http://neptune.netimages.com/~chile/hottest.html

Johnny's Pepper Page (chile-related information)
http://members.tripod.com/~Juanito/chiles.html

Smoke N' Mirrors Hot Sauce Database
http://www.netjammer.com/hotsauce/

Tough Love Chile Company (habañero seeds)
http://www.powernet.net/~chilehed1/

Transcendental Capsaicinophilic Society
http://www.io.com/~m101/tcs/

Index of hot sauce manufacturers, retail sources, restaurants, festivals, and web sites.